How To Find Your
FAMILY ROOTS
and Write Your
FAMILY
HISTORY

by
William Latham
an
Cindy Higgins

SANTA
MONICA
PRESS

SANTA MONICA PRESS LLC
P.O. Box 1076
Santa Monica, CA 90406
1-800-784-9553
www.santamonicapress.com

Printed in the United States

Santa Monica Press books are available at special quantity discounts when purchased in bulk by corporations, organizations or groups. Please call our Special Sales department at 1-800-784-9553.

This book is intended to provide general information. The publisher, author, distributor, and copyright owner are not engaged in rendering legal or other professional advice and services, and are not liable or responsible to any person or group with respect to any loss caused or alleged to be caused by the information found in this book.

This is a revised edition of How to Find Your Family Roots ©1994

Library of Congress Cataloging-in-Publication Data

Latham, William, 1942–
    How to find your family roots and write your family history / by William Latham and Cindy Higgins.
        p.   cm.
    Includes bibliographical references.
    ISBN 1-891661-12-4
        1. Genealogy. 2. United States—Genealogy—Handbooks, manuals, etc. I. Higgins, Cindy, 1956–II. Title

CS16. L39 2000
929.1—dc21   99-059931

Book and cover design by **cooldog**design

Contents

Introduction
The Excitement of Finding Your Family Roots   9
Definition and History of Genealogy
What You Will Accomplish

Chapter One
A Brief History of America's Immigrants   15
From Many Lands, for Many Reasons
The Harrowing Voyage Across the Ocean
Crossing the Country

Chapter Two
Starting Your Search for Your Family Roots   19
Tools of the Trade
Organizing Your Research Material

Chapter Three
Names, Relationships, and Dates: Early Keys to Your Search 27
Names
Name Origins and Meaning
Did Your Ancestor Change Names?
How to Search for a Changed Name
Relationships
Dates

Chapter Four
You and Your Family: Your Most Important Resources   41
Begin with Yourself
The Next Step—Your Family Members
Finding Relics in the Attic and Basement

Chapter *Five*
Using Computers for Genealogical Searches   53
Internet Searches
E-Mail, Mailing Lists, and Newsgroups
World Wide Web
Genealogy Software

Chapter *Six*
The Tremendous Riches of Libraries   61
Take Advantage of Your Local Library
What to Ask Librarians
Libraries of Special Genealogical Significance
What You Can Find in Libraries
Genealogical Publishers and Booksellers
Genealogical Societies

Chapter *Seven*
Church Records and Cemeteries   79
Western Civilization's Record Keepers
How to Use Church Records
How to Obtain Church Records
Cemeteries
Recording Tombstone Information

Chapter *Eight*
Local and State Records   89
A Word About Primary Sources
Researching Primary Source Records
First Steps
Vital Documents
Property Records
Probate Records

Chapter Nine
Federal Government Research Sources   99

The National Archives
Census Records
Non-population Censuses
Military Records
Service Records
Veteran Pensions
Bounty Land Grants
Homestead Files and Other Land Transactions
Passenger Lists and Naturalization Records
Social Security Records
Passports
Federal Bureau of Investigation Records
Hiring a Professional Genealogist—The Right Decision for You?

Chapter Ten
Searching for Ancestors in Foreign Countries   125

List of Sources, Country by Country

Chapter Elev
Special Genealogical Challenges   61

Adoptees
African Americans
Hispanic Americans
Jewish Americans
Native Americans
Women

Chapter Twelve
Writing Your Family History   173

Getting Started
How to Present Your Information

Chapter Thirteen

**Incorporating the Art of Storytelling Into
Your Family History Writing**   183

Storytelling Techniques
Writing About People Alive Today
Writing About Ancestors
Break Into Song
Adding Personality
Insert Yourself
From Start to Finish or . . . ?
Endings

Chapter Fourteen

Using History in Family History Writing   195

History Adds Clarification
History Provides a Setting
History Fleshes Out "Bare Bones" Story Areas
History Gives Pizzazz
Easy History Sources
Know What You are Writing About

Chapter Fifteen

Information Presentation   209

Determine Your Ethical Stance
Avoid Faulty Reasoning
Consider the Source
Prove It! And Prove It Again! And Again!
Definitions
Documentation
Source Citation
Bibliographies

Chapter Sixteen

Editing Your Writing   221

Concept Editing
Line Editing

Chapter Seventeen
Visual Accents   **227**

Paragraph Typography
Photographs
Beyond Photographs
Line Art
Charts
Illustration Placement

Chapter Eighteen
Packaging the Story   **235**

Contents
Frontmatter
Backmatter
Camera Ready?
Printer Types and Estimates
Paper
Page Placement
Binding
Cover
How Many to Print?
Preserving Family Histories

Chapter Nineteen
Sharing Your Family History   **253**

Celebrate Your Success with a Family Reunion
Reunion Activities
Countdown to the Reunion
Be Prepared

Appendix   **257**

State Repositories (Including public libraries, historical
  society libraries, and archives)
Vital Records (United States and Canada)
Genealogical Magazines, E-Zines, and Web Sites
Genealogical Publishers
Bibliography

THE EXCITEMENT OF FINDING YOUR FAMILY ROOTS

*H*ave you ever wondered whether one of your ancestors was a famous person? A president, or even a King or a Queen? Perhaps your last name is Washington, and you've always thought that perhaps you were a distant relative of the father of our country. If you've shown a flair for painting or writing, maybe you've fantasized that you inherited your talent from a talented ancestor.

Certainly the heritage of each and every one of us is a fascinating topic. Who hasn't dreamed of origins, or people living in another place, in another time? Who hasn't seen an old photograph of a person to whom they bear a striking resemblance and thought, "I wonder whether. . . ?"

In this book, we will show you how the process of finding your family roots—known as "genealogy"—can act as a kind of time machine or magic carpet that allows you to travel back into the past. Once there, you can find information that has helped to shape you —not only in terms of your physical appearance, but your personality, beliefs, habits, and skills as well. Additionally, this search for your roots will take you through time and space, from century to century and from state to state or even exotic country to country. Your search will give you a greater sense of exactly how you fit into this giant web of people and places that we call the history of mankind. And, what's more, we'll show you how to do all of this in a simple, easy, and inexpensive manner.

How to Find Your Family Roots is not an academic report filled with complicated research techniques and impossible suggestions and instructions. Instead, it is written for people like you who are naturally curious. People who care about their family and their heritage and want to find valuable information to share with other family members and pass it on to future generations. You'll discover that it's not only easy to find out a great deal of information about your family roots, it's also a lot of fun! Think of it like a giant jigsaw puzzle, of which you, your family, and your ancestors are the pieces!!

DEFINITION AND HISTORY OF GENEALOGY

The term "genealogy" actually comes from two Greek works: "genea," which means "race" or "family"; and "logia," which means "science" or "study of." When we speak of genealogy, we are really talking about the study of the descent of a person or of a family.

The science of genealogy is as old as the Bible, which itself serves as the first written example of genealogy. Ancient civilizations, such as the Greeks, showed a keen interest in genealogy—as displayed in the works of Homer and the plays of Aeschylus and Euripides. Another early use of genealogy was to prove that a person was descended from certain gods and goddesses or from rulers. Later, rulers or the upper classes actively pursued genealogical interests. That changed in the sixteenth century when extensive written records began to be kept, thus making it far easier for ordinary citizens to trace their lineage.

Any way you look at it, interest in man's lineage is as old as civilized man himself.

WHAT YOU WILL ACCOMPLISH

As you begin the task of unraveling the mystery of your family's origin, you will learn a great deal about the history of both America and the world, as well as about geography, people and their lifestyles, and most importantly, yourself-who you are and where you come from.

Ideally, you should be able to trace your roots back to the original paternal and maternal immigrants of your family or maybe even further than that. If you are able to do this, you will know your complete American genealogy and you should congratulate yourself—most people do not know this much about their family. Your next step would be to try and trace your lineage to the forefathers of your family's original immigrants, to those who were born and those who died in some far away country hundreds of years ago. Finally, you will take whatever information you have gathered and write a letter, report, or even a book about your discoveries. Some enthusiasts even form a family organization that meets once or twice a year, bringing together relatives that they have never met or possibly didn't even know existed.

But even if you are only able to go back two or three generations, even if you only come up with a handful of dates, names and places, you will have accomplished a great deal, something of which you can be especially proud. Why? Because you will have the satisfaction of knowing that you have set up a solid foundation for the future generations of your family. You will have set a precedent that will surely inspire one of your descendants to pick up the ball and continue the project you started. Additionally, by providing a written record of your lineage, you will give those around you and those who will follow in your footsteps immeasurable joy in knowing just who they are and where they come from.

Perhaps we're getting a little too serious here. The main thing you must keep in mind while tracing your family tree is to have fun! Because it's not about how far back you are able to go or how complete a family history you are able to put together. No, it's really about getting in touch with relatives you haven't talked to in a long time or have never even met. It's about finding long lost mementos and hearing old family tales that have been buried in the memories of your older relatives for years and years because nobody was ever truly interested enough to ask them to tell these stories. It's about all of this and much, much more. . . .

And remember, the sooner you get started, the better. Your relatives are not getting any younger, and once they are gone, their memories and their stories will go with them. Don't let time pass you by, leaving you in the unenviable position of kicking yourself while you cry, "If only I would've talked to him while he was alive!" So what are you waiting for? Let's begin your search for your family roots!

Chapter One

A BRIEF HISTORY OF AMERICA'S IMMIGRANTS

FROM MANY LANDS, FOR MANY REASONS

*B*eginning with those who sailed to America aboard the Mayflower in 1620, the first immigrants who came to our country were primarily from England. In the early part of the eighteenth century, the Germans, Scottish, and Irish began crossing over, and by the end of the 1700s, close to five million people lived in the United States. With the exception of three-quarters of a million black African slaves, the vast majority of the people living in the United States at this time were from one of these four original countries.

By the mid-1800s, people from all over the world, including Ireland, France, Switzerland, China, and Japan, began immigrating to the United States. And between 1880 and the early part of the twentieth century, over 15 million southern and eastern Europeans came to better their lives in America.

Aside from the economic opportunities, immigrants sought out America as a refuge from religious persecution, political oppression, and a host of other reasons—including wanderlust and the attraction of the unknown.

THE HARROWING VOYAGE ACROSS THE OCEAN

Europeans left from a handful of sea ports. At these seedy ports, many tried to take advantage of the travelers embarking on their rough, uncomfortable voyage, crammed together with others in tiny cabins. Dangers, ranging from pirates who roamed the open seas, to disease and fierce storms that pounded the planks of the ships, also contributed to the overall hardship of the journey.

The length of the voyages varied from a little over a month to well over four months, bringing even more uncertainty to the travelers. At times, groups of ships would sail together. Other times, however, days would pass without another ship in sight.

Once the immigrants set foot on American soil, most with less than 25 dollars in their pockets, they forgot the trip hardships, and looked forward to new opportunities. Before Ellis Island was built in 1892, immigrants were processed at Castle Garden, located at the far tip of Manhattan. Asian immigrants were processed at the Pacific Mail Steamship Company warehouse in San Francisco, but after 1910 they were welcomed at Angel Island in San Francisco Bay.

CROSSING THE COUNTRY

Once landed on the east coast of America, early immigrants typically settled in one of two places—Massachusetts and Virginia. By the mid-seventeenth century, immigrants from an assortment of countries would often take uncomfortable, even punishing stagecoach rides on the King's Highway to Philadelphia, Pennsylvania. Many would then continue on to Norfolk, Virginia, and even as far south as Charleston, South Carolina. In later years, an immigrant could get on a stage coach in Philadelphia and take the Great Road out west toward Kentucky, which became a state in 1792.

In 1803, U.S. settlement had reached 17 million and extended to the Missouri River. The introduction of steamboats, hard surfaced toll roads, and canals helped tie the nation together, as did the first railway that began operation in 1830. Wherever railroad tracks were laid, cities sprang up.

Thirty years after the Revolutionary War, the industrial revolution was in full force. Factory hands couldn't keep up with work demands, so workers streamed in from other countries to fill the need. One million came from famine-ravaged Ireland between 1840 and 1850 to toil up to fifteen hours a day in hazardous buildings.

Elsewhere, the 1849 Gold Rush was followed ten years later by a strike in Colorado, and another in Nevada at the Comstock Lode. Miners also went to Montana, Idaho, and the Black hills of South Dakota, thus advancing settlement in the West.

The Homestead Act passed by Congress in 1862 also attracted thousands of settlers, eager to obtain title to 160 free acres of public land, provided they lived there five years and made improvements.

While the roads were tough and the journey arduous, our forefathers not only survived, but triumphed with a dignity and pride that has since gone on to be associated with the word, "American."

Chapter Two

STARTING YOUR SEARCH FOR YOUR FAMILY ROOTS

TOOLS OF THE TRADE

$\mathcal{T}$he only tools really required when you begin searching out your family roots are a notepad and pen or pencil. The notepad is so you can jot down notes, thoughts, hints, tips, and the like. Valuable information can be obtained at any time, in any place. You'll want to have a place to write the facts as opposed to relying on your memory. You may also want to use a separate notebook as your Research Log in which you list sources that you have examined. This way you won't repeat your research.

If interviewing people, you might want to use a small tape recorder. Recorders eliminate the need to take copious notes during interviews and are unobtrusive. If you are comfortable with computers, you might want to purchase a digital recorder that allows you to enter your notes directly onto your computer.

On the subject of computers, software now makes stockpiling, retrieving, and displaying data easy. Once input, information can be sorted by names and relationships, numbered using genealogical systems, placed in a variety of charts, and even transferred to a word processing program. For more information on recording software, see *Chapter Five: Using Computers for Genealogical Searches.*

ORGANIZING YOUR RESEARCH MATERIAL

As you begin searching your family roots, you will undoubtedly begin to gather a great deal of material, ranging from charts and documents to mementos and family photographs. To keep track of everything, you need some type of filing system. Without a system, you will end up with a morass of notes and papers that will make it difficult for you to find necessary items crucial to continuing your search.

Before getting into the particulars of a filing system, first let's go over the major documents with which you will be working. One is the Ancestral

Chart (also known as a Pedigree Chart), the other is the Family Group Chart.

ANCESTRAL CHARTS

An ancestral chart (*see Figure 1, next page*) is the record of direct ancestors. It's grandparents and great-grandparents, not siblings, uncles, or cousins. The ancestral line moves backward in time and identifies succeeding ancestors by generation. The first ancestral chart you fill out will go back four generations, to approximately the middle of the 1800s. As you move along in your search, you fill out the ancestral chart to mark your progress. If doing this on paper charts, it is a good idea to fill out this chart in pencil to make changes, if necessary.

The standard format to follow is to start with yourself, record each member's full name, placing every letter of each surname in capitals. For example, ADAMS. Alice Jill.

Next, write the month, day, and year this person was born (e.g., March 18, 1953). After that comes the place of birth, which should include the city, state, and county, if possible. Use the standard two-letter abbreviation for the state if you wish. Continue this format for the dates and places of marriages and deaths. If unsure about a fact, place a question mark in parenthesis following the questionable information.

NUMBERING SYSTEM

When filling out ancestral charts (*see Figure 1*), assign each member a number. Then, all materials that

Figure 1: ANCESTRAL CHART (THREE GENERATION)

4

Name: ADAMS, Joseph
Born: April 5, 1905
Place: Chicago, IL
Married: October 7, 1927
Place: Chicago, IL
Died: July 17, 1977
Place: Kansas City, MO

2

Name: ADAMS, John L.
Born: June 9, 1930
Place: Kansas City, MO
Married: May 10, 1955
Place: Kansas City, MO
Died: July 17, 1989
Place: Phoenix, AZ

5

Name: BARR, Mary Alice
Born: June 27, 1910
Place: Chicago, IL
Married: October 7, 1927
Place: Chicago, IL
Died: February 3, 1962
Place: Kansas City, MO

1

Name: ADAMS, Alice Jill
Born: March 18, 1953
Place: Kansas City, MO
Married: May 14, 1973
Place: Santa Monica, CA

6

Name: TULLEY, Walter
Born: January 15, 1899
Place: Boston, MA
Married: June 23, 1937
Place: Detroit, MI
Died: September 8, 1965
Place: Dallas, TX

3

Name: TULLEY, Eunice
Born: April 1, 1938
Place: Detroit, MI
Married: October 3, 1955
Place: Kansas City, MO

7

Name: CLARK, Lucy Ann
Born: March 30, 1918
Place: Detroit, MI
Married: June 23, 1937
Place: Detroit, MI
Married: May 14, 1969
Place: Santa Monica, CA

relate to individual family members will be filed under this same number. The easiest way to go about doing this is to begin with yourself, assigning the number 1 to your name. Number 2 will then go to your father, number 3 to your mother, and so on. To further facilitate your records, only assign even numbers to males, and odd numbers to females. Therefore, number 4 will be your paternal grandfather (your father's father), number 5 your paternal grandmother (your father's mother), number 6 your maternal grandfather (your mother's father), number 7 your maternal grandmother (your mother's mother), etc. While this may initially be slightly confusing, in the long run you will find that it actually makes your record keeping exceedingly clear.

FAMILY GROUP CHART

The other standard genealogical form is the family group chart (*see Figure 2, next page*). It focuses on one nuclear family and lists a husband, wife, and any children, with blanks for names, dates, places, residences, and other data. When filling out these charts, keep in mind that two or even three marriages per individual were not uncommon in earlier times. Rougher lifestyles and primitive medicine often led to the early deaths of one partner or another. In instances of multiple marriages, keep a separate family group chart for each marriage.

These charts also provide a record of sources used to obtain information. Not only will this help you, but it is useful for others who want to verify the research and use it as a starting point to find other information. When recording, follow genealogical style. That means,

Figure 2: Family Group Chart

Husband's Code Number: ____

Husband	Wife

Name: _____

Date of Birth: _____

Place of Birth: _____

Father's Name: _____

Mother's Name: _____

Date of Marriage: _____

Place of Marriage: _____

Date of Death: _____

Place of Death: _____

Children

Name	Born	Place	Died	Place

Family Residences

City	County	State	Dates

record women's maiden names for a surname, and, if the name is not known, leave the space for a last name blank. For dates, use day, month, and year (e.g., 27 Feb 1880). This eliminates the need for a comma. Places are recorded by city, county, and state (Calveras, Marin, California) with the word "county" omitted.

Most importantly, be extremely accurate when placing information onto these charts. Any error could prove to be costly, leading you into hours of research that will ultimately prove to be needless and unwarranted. If, for instance, you place a wrong first name for one of the children, you could begin searching somebody's life who isn't even a member of your family. Always check and double-check your facts and figures.

FILING SYSTEM

Now we come to the final portion of organization. Because each family group chart is tagged with the number of the husband (or head of the family), the chart will be filed according to the numerical sequence 2, 4, 6, 8, 10. . . (with the possible addition of number 1 if the genealogist himself is the head of the family).

Besides family group chart files, keep a miscellaneous file for smaller files arranged by family group chart code numbers. It will hold photographs, diaries, wills, newspaper clippings and anything else that pertains to a certain family member. This file ensures that you don't end up with piles of information in bits and pieces.

You may also want to keep a file titled "Dead End" for any leads and information sources that ultimately led nowhere. You never know when such information may come into play, and keeping this research in one place makes it easy to find should you suddenly have use for it.

Let's go through and see how your filing system and family group charts operate. Say that you want to look up all the information that you have collected about your paternal grandfather (your father's father). To begin, you will notice that on the ancestral chart, he has been assigned the number of 4. You would then go to the family group chart also numbered 4, and the miscellaneous file also marked with the number 4.

If, for instance, you wanted to look up your paternal grandmother's brothers and sisters, you would go to the family group chart numbered 10. Why? Because, as you can see from the ancestral chart, your paternal grandmother's father has been assigned the number 10, and therefore all information about your grandmother's brothers and sisters will be contained on the family group chart that corresponds with your grandmother's father's code number, or number 10.

This system is efficient and simple once you get going. And that's exactly what you are now prepared to do. With an excellent record-keeping system at your disposal, you are now ready to plunge ahead into the exciting world of "ancestor hunting." So, with this out of the way, let's go. . . .

Chapter Three

NAMES, RELATIONSHIPS, AND DATES: EARLY KEYS TO YOUR SEARCH

NAMES

*Y*our family name is the fundamental element of your genealogical quest. Like a fingerprint, a name is a personal marking that offers the first clue as to who you are and where you came from. By understanding the origin, history, and meaning of names, you will be able to uncover a remarkable amount of information— the town where an ancestor was born, his or her occupation, religion, cultural times, class status, and even personality or physical characteristics!

NAME ORIGINS AND MEANING

The original Anglo-Saxon names had little or no meaning 5,000 years ago. Many names, such as Clovis and Begga, did not make a distinction between males and females. But with the Norman Conquest of 1066, the English and Europeans began using the Norman names— Richard, Robert, etc.—that remain familiar to us now.

The Normans only used a handful of names and, with an increasing population, people living in the Middle Ages found themselves running short of name choices. At this point, the Church stepped in and began suggesting that parents use saints' names for their newborns, and so Stephen, Elizabeth, Katherine, and others immediately became popular. It was also at this time that people began to add descriptions to their names to distinguish themselves from family, friends, neighbors, and fellow townspeople with the same name. These descriptions usually had to do with an individual's physical characteristics or the place where they lived, such as Robert the Bald or John of the Glen.

By the fifteenth century, surnames had become common and, as with given names, they often described what someone looked like or where they lived. If Richard was not a tall man, he could have been called Richard Short. Everard, who lived in Hungerford, was known as Everard de Hungerford. Personal characteristics and occupations also began to be reflected in a person's name. Weaver, Farmer, Miller, Cooper, and Baker were common surnames denoting occupations.

Finally, relationships were often designated within surnames through the practice known as patronymics. Such names point out that an individual was the son or descendant of a particular person, hence "O" for the Irish, "Ben" (Hebrew), "de" (French), "Mc" and "Mac" (Scottish), and plain old "son" attached to a name end for the English. For example, MacGregor is Scottish for "the son of Gregory," Johnson is "the son of John," while Mendelssohn is German for the "son of Mendel." However, when patronymics first began to be used, the surname would change with every generation. Thus, John, the son of Peter would be called John Peterson. But John's son, Robert, would be known as Robert Johnson. Henry V came along and effectively put an end to this confusing practice when, in 1413, he ordered that everyone begin using surnames on all legal documents. By the middle of the sixteenth century, family names had become stabilized. Surnames derived from patronymics remained the same from generation to generation.

Many excellent books deal exclusively with the history of names, or "onomatology." J. N. Hook's *Family Names: How Our Surnames Came to America*, Elsdon C. Smith's American Surnames, and P. H. Reaney's *Dictionary of British Surnames* are all highly recommended. Generally, surname origin books are found in your library's reference section or on library shelves in the 929 Dewey Decimal section.

Did Your Ancestor Change Names?

It is estimated that more than 1.5 million last names are currently used in the United States. This may sound like a large number, but it is relatively small when you think about the tremendous amount of immigrants who have brought numbers of Western and Eastern European names into the country.

Why is this? Basically, because immigrants to this country often changed their name—or were given a new name—when they entered the United States. This resulted in many new citizens taking similar names. In fact, the most common names in America today—Smith, Jones, Johnson, Brown—are virtually the same as they were around the time of the American Revolution. The name "Smith" provides a good example of how this worked. Immigrants from different countries whose name meant "blacksmith"—for example, the German "Schmidt" or the Italian "Ferraro"—adopted the name "Smith" when they reached the shores of America. Thus, what was already a popular, although variously spelled and pronounced, name in many countries was suddenly funneled into one name in America. The result was an enormous amount of people having the same name and making that name extraordinarily popular for succeeding generations.

The changing of an immigrant's name was done for a variety of reasons. One was to "Americanize" a name.

For instance, many German immigrants discovered that Americans had trouble pronouncing their names, and so "Koch" became "Cook" and "Albrecht" became "Allbright."

It was even more common for the name change to be a result of a decision made by an immigration official, especially in the case of Polish immigrants. Someone from Poland with a name such as "Marcizszewski" would come through, and out of confusion or simply laziness, the immigration official would change the spelling to the closest English pronunciation he could come up with on the spot, such as "Muskie." Welfare agencies and church officials back in an immigrants' native country also often changed spelling, as did our ancestors themselves. Daniel Boone, for example, was known to have signed his name "Bone" and "Boon" in addition to the spelling we are familiar with, "Boone." Federal census takers also proved inept at recording correct name spelling, and the census of 1790 finds even simple names spelled dozens of ways. Here are examples of common names and the variations you might encounter if you were searching for one of them:

Brown: Bronn, Broons, Broune, Browne
Bailey: Bailie, Bailly, Baillie, Baily, Baley
Madison: Maddison, Matheson, Matsen, Matson, Mattison, Mattson
Meyer: Mayer, Meier, Meyers, Mier, Myer
Reynolds: Ranals, Rehnholds, Reynull, Rynolds

While name variants may not at first seem to be important, they prove crucial when searching for family roots. Remember, you will be looking through all kinds of public records. If you aren't aware of the different spellings of your ancestors' surnames, you may well overlook key pieces of information that could unlock the door that leads to a whole branch of your family tree.

How to Search for a Changed Name

Searching for ancestors would be easier if the spelling of last names remained consistent throughout the centuries, but unfortunately that is not the case. Don't despair, though, for this can be overcome. The first thing to do is to think of all the ways you can possibly spell your last name. For instance, if your last name is "Kane," you might write "Cain," "Cane," "Caine," "Kain," "Kaine," and "Kaines." Sometimes, saying your name out loud a few times will help you think of other possibilities. Try also to mispronounce your name to see whether that raises additional spellings. And remember to include the spellings and pronunciations that other people have mistakenly used during your lifetime.

Once you begin actively searching for your family roots, you will discover ways to find out either your ancestor's original name or a spelling variant. In cemeteries, you'll often find the original, pre-immigration surname on the tombstone, as many of our ancestors chose to be buried with their original name as opposed to the one they either adopted or were forced to adopt upon landing in the United States. Death certificates might also contain an ancestor's original name. If you by chance come across several death certificates from

Figure 3: OCCUPATIONAL NAME CHANGES

ENGLISH	FRENCH	GERMAN	ITALIAN	POLISH
Baker	Boulanger	Becker	Fornari	Piekarz
Carpenter	Charpentier	Schreiner	Martello	Cieslak
Farmer	Gagnon	Bauer		Kmiec
Fisher		Fischer	Pisciolo	Ryback
Miller	Meunier	Muller	Farina	
Priest		Pabst	Prete	Kaplan
Shepherd	Berger	Schaefer	Pecora	
Taylor	Tailleur	Schneider	Sartori	Krawczyk

members of one family, and one certificate contains a different spelling of—or even a completely different—last name, don't dismiss it as a clerical error. That ancestor may have given you a valuable clue through his or her choice to be buried with his original name.

One of the most common occurrences of name changes can be seen with occupational names. If you or one of your ancestors has this type of name, the name change may be easy to identify. Here are several examples:

You might be thinking that coming up with a half-dozen ways to spell your name will only make your search that much more complicated. It won't. You will have other information available, such as birth dates, birth places, death dates, burial places, etc., which will help you narrow your search a great deal. *The Directory of Family Associations* (Elizabeth Petty Bentley, Baltimore: Genealogical Publishing, 1996) contains more than 6,500 family name associations in the U.S. The Pipkin family, for instance, may have their own newsletter or sponsor a family reunion. This information can also be found in the annual *Everton's Genealogical Helper* devoted to family associations. You may want to contact one of these distant family members and determine how you connect!

RELATIONSHIPS

While relationships to our parents, brothers, sister, and children are relatively simple to understand, and while most of us have a firm grasp of our relationship to cousins, aunts, uncles, and grandparents, more distant relationships can get confusing. Yet, when searching for your family's roots, you must comprehend relationships if you expect to put together an accurate family tree. Additionally, if you erroneously claim an individual as your ancestors, and then begin to trace his roots, you will have wasted a great deal of time and energy. Here are a few tips and hints that may help clear up the relationships puzzle:

1) The first thing you should know about relationships is the distinction between "direct" ancestors and "collateral" relatives. A direct ancestor's name will appear on your ancestral chart—your father, mother, grandparents, or great-grandparents. A collateral relative will only appear on family group charts as either brothers or sisters of your direct relatives, or as descendants of your aunts and uncles.

2) Aside from direct and collateral relationships, there are also "in-laws," and "step," "half," and

"adoptive" relationships. "In-laws" are related by marriage; they are the ancestors and relatives of a spouse. "Step" relationships occur when a man or woman with children remarries. If a woman with a boy remarries a man who has no children, then the man becomes the boy's stepfather, and all of the man's relatives become step relatives to the boy. If the woman and the man have a daughter together, the new baby girl becomes a "half" sister to the little boy. When researching adoptive situations, realize that, rightly or wrongly, many hereditary and lineage societies will not accept adopted descendants as members, even though they may have all the legal rights of heirs.

3) To simplify your records, succeeding generations of great-grandparents should be identified as 2nd great-grandfather (or grandmother), 3rd great-grandfather, etc. Grandsons and granddaughters should also be identified by this same system, as 2nd great-grandson (or granddaughter), 3rd great-grandson, and so forth.

4) A first cousin, obviously, is the child of your uncle or aunt. The word "cousin" takes on a different meaning when applied to someone more remotely related who still shares a common ancestor. In these instances, terms such as second cousin and third cousin, or third cousin once removed begin to enter into the genealogical picture. Your first cousin's child is your first cousin once removed. The child of your first cousin

once removed is your first cousin twice removed, and so forth. Now, your second cousin is the grandchild of your grandparents' brothers or sisters (your "great-aunts" or "great-uncles"). Your second cousin's child is your second cousin once removed, and that person's child is your second cousin twice removed. Your third cousin? That person is your great-grandparent's brother's or sister's great-grandchild. And, if your third cousin has a child, that person is your third cousin once removed, and so forth.

5) Cousin relationships become even more confusing as you go back into history. During the seventeenth century, for instance, the term "cousin" was applied to any relative who wasn't a brother, sister, son, or daughter. Grandchildren, nephews and nieces, uncles and aunts—those relatives were often referred to as "cousins" in wills and other legal documents. Similarly, stepchildren (a spouse's child by a former marriage) were often referred to as a "son-in-law" or "daughter-in-law," while "son" and "daughter" were often used in place of the twentieth century meaning we assign the terms "son-in-law" and "daughter-in-law."

6) "Brother" can also be a tricky term in historical documents. Aside from the definition we tend to use—that of a blood brother, or one who shares the same parents as ourselves—"brother" often means "brother-in-law," "step-brother," or

a church "brother." Likewise, "father" and "mother" often stood for the terms we use for "father-in-law," "mother-in-law," "step-father," or "stepmother." Redflag the terms "Junior" and "Senior," because they do not necessarily mean father and son. They also can mean that two people had the same name and there was a difference in their ages. In earlier times, this term was used for uncles and nephews, and, sometimes, for two people not related at all!

7) The last sources of confusion that may come across as you travel back through the centuries concerns the use of "Mrs." This title often stood for "Mistriss," a term of social distinction for a woman who may or may not have been married.

When researching family roots, make sure that you pay close attention to the terms used to describe relationships in wills, birth and death certificates, and other legal documents. Never take anything at face value. Look at other familial records for collaboration before accepting a new member into your genealogical family.

DATES

When searching through records that refer to any year before 1752, you might come across dates that look peculiar. Perhaps the most common puzzler is the appearance of "Old Style" or "New Style" (often abbreviated to O.S. and N.S.) following a date, and the practice known as "double dating." This term refers to the custom of using two years when citing a date of birth or death. For instance, if you were searching for George Washington's date of birth, you might find a record that has the date written as February 11, 1731/2. Or, you might see it elsewhere as February 11, 1731, Old Style or February 22, 1732, New Style.

Double dating, Old Style, and New Style occur because of a change originally made to the calendar in 1582, which the English adopted in 1752. Before 1582, the Julian calendar—established by Julius Caesar in 46 B.C.—was the favored calendar of the Christian world. According to this calendar, the year was divided into 364 days, and every fourth (or leap) year there would be an extra day. However, in 1582, it was discovered that every 400 years the Julian calendar was three days ahead of the actual time as dictated by the earth's revolution around the sun. By 1582, this translated into ten extra days. If this remained unchecked, the months of the year and the seasons that we normally associate with them—for instance August with summer or February with winter—would no longer match. More importantly, the date of the vernal equinox had shifted from March 21 to March 11, and the dates for Easter had been thrown out of sorts. Appropriately, the Roman Catholic countries, in accordance with a decree from Pope Gregory XII, pushed their calendars ahead by ten days.

While moving the date up ten days solved the problem of matching the new, or Gregorian, calendar with that of the earth's, it still did nothing to fix the problem of gaining 3 days every 400 years. The Gregorian calendar solved this problem by mandating that years ending in hundreds be leap years only if divisible by 400. Confused? To put it simply, in the years 1700, 1800, and 1900—normally leap years—the extra day was not added, while the year 2,000 will remain a leap year. This way, those pesky three extra days every four hundred years will be kept in check. Even more importantly, the Gregorian calendar also established January 1 as the New Year, instead of the traditional Christina date of March 25.

It took the more conservative English until the beginning of September in 1752 to implement the Gregorian calendar. By this point, the Julian (or Old Style) calendar was eleven days ahead of the Gregorian (or New Style) calendar. So, when the switch was made on September 2, 1752, the following day suddenly became September 14, 1752. This change effectively made all persons born before this date 11 days older. If a baby was born on September 2 (according to the Old Style calendar) he or she would be twelve days old when waking up the following day, September 14 (according to the New Style calendar). It should be noted that when Parliament approved of using the Gregorian calendar, there was a great deal of public unrest, including several riots. People apparently thought the government was stealing away eleven days of their lives!

Because of these changes, records having to do with the months of January, February, and March before 1752 will often use double dates, for example, March 18, 1675/76. This may seem confusing, but you must remember that the Old Style calendar considered January, February, and most of March to be part of the preceding year, whereas the New Style calendar made January 1 the New Year. For example, February 22, 1748 (Old Style) is the same as February 11, 1749 (New Style).

In some instances, records will explicitly refer to either the Old Style calendar or the New Style calendar, for instance, March 18, 1676 New Style. You should also be wary of records before 1752 that refer to the month not by name, but with a number. If a date is written as 18, 3rd month, 1675, it is most likely referring to May 18, 1675, as it is using March as the first month of the year.

Awareness of the eleven day differential and the change in the date of the New Year will help you whenever you come across discrepancies in birth and death records. When one record has the birth date of an ancestor occurring eleven days earlier than another record, you can be sure that the record with the earlier date was based on the Old Style calendar. Similarly, if one record claims that an ancestor of yours gave birth to a son on April 15, 1650, and another record indicates that she also gave birth to a daughter on March 16, 1650, the latter record used the Old Style calendar, and that the daughter was actually born on March 5, 1651.

Lastly, while you may never encounter unusual dating practices in your own research, this information still provides a valuable lesson on the importance of using every available resource at your disposal when tracing your family roots. You must be able to keep enough of an open mind to find that one clue, that one valuable piece of information, that solves a riddle and allows you to bring your search to yet another succeeding generation instead of stopping right then and there. Always be curious!

Chapter Four

You and Your Family: Your Most Important Resources

Begin with Yourself

When beginning the search for your family roots, you must commence the hunt with an examination of yourself. You are the base of your ultimate family tree. Besides, you are obviously the easiest subject to research!

Start by filling out the ancestral chart as far back as you can go with the knowledge you have at your immediate disposal, and then move on to your family group charts. Try to always backtrack from the present to the past in all research for more accurate reporting.

You may have the urge to skip this portion of the research process, mistakenly thinking that you know this so well that you can write it all any time. That is the wrong attitude to have at this point. Instead, welcome the opportunity to get practice in research itself, recording facts, and even verifying them in some instances.

Obtain accurate information! Any wrong information on your part at this point could lead you on an erroneous path that will take you far from where you want to be. Don't include any information that you *think* is correct. Unless you are positive about a fact, always compare it with as many references as you can before declaring it to be true.

Additionally, also write down family anecdotes, accomplishments, personality quirks. . . .in general, anything that strikes you as being interesting in any way. If all you record are simple facts such as birthday and place names, you will end up with a dry, boring family history. On the other hand, little slices of life, sad and funny tales about family members, and other tidbits will help make your final family history a fascinating report to read.

The Next Step—Your Family Members

A standard genealogical practice is to get as close to the source as possible when verifying facts. By beginning with sources who are alive, you will save time, energy, and just as importantly, you may discover new, rewarding relationships. If the person you are researching is no longer living, try to communicate with a living person who was closest to that person. If, for example, you wanted to find out something about your great paternal grandfather's brothers and sister, you could go to your paternal grandfather or one of his brothers or sisters to find out the information. If your grandfather and his brothers and sisters are no longer living, you could go to your father or one of your aunts or uncles. In cases involving family members with whom you are not on good terms, ask another family member who knows both of you to do the interviewing for you—but remember that this can only be considered secondhand information.

Interviewing Family Members in Person

After you have contacted your relative by mail or phone and informed them of the project and your desire to interview them, set up a time to meet that is convenient for them. Here are a few guidelines for interviewing:

1) Try to conduct the interview in a one-on-one setting. However, if another relative would like to be present at the interview, by all means allow that person to do so-two people talking about the past often trigger memories within each other.

2) Bring a tape recorder if at all possible. Small, portable tape recorders allow you to concentrate on what the person is saying, rather than

racing to write every word that comes out of his or her mouth. Plus, you'll have a valuable heirloom—a permanent record of an in-depth conversation with a relative for succeeding generations to hear. If you have access to a video camera, you may want to videotape the interview. Set the camera on a tripod, focus on the subject, press the record button, and begin asking questions.

3) Prepare a list of questions on a few sheets of paper. When writing the questions, try to order them in such a way that one question leads naturally into the next. For instance, if you want to know about one relative in particular, keep all of your questions about this relative—when he was born, where he lived, and other vital statistics—together, so that the interview does not jump back and forth from person to person, place to place, and decade to decade. Also, avoid questions that encourage a simple "yes" or "no" answer.

Opening questions that might be asked of an ancestor from another country could include: Where were you born? When did you arrive in this country? Did your family change their last name when they came to the United States? Where did your family first settle upon their arrival? What was life like during those first few years in America? Do you remember any stories about those years? What type of work did your father do?. . . .

4) LISTEN. Let the person you are interviewing do the talking. Never interrupt, and don't assume someone has finished just because they pause for a moment. Always wait for the person to tell you he or she is finished, or wait for a substantial pause before you ask your next question. If a relative seems to be wandering, talking about things you haven't asked about, by all means let the relative talk. It is very likely that the person will come up with an interesting fact about or insight into your roots. If he or she mentions something in passing that you would like to know more about, jot it down on a piece of paper, and when the person is done talking, you can go back and ask about this fact.

5) Phrase questions in a manner that avoids any bias on your part. That is, instead of asking, "Your Uncle Ralph was born in New Orleans, right?" Say "Where was your Uncle Ralph born?"

6) Don't make the interview last too long. One or two hours should be the maximum amount of time you should impose on your subject at any one sitting. By all means, arrange for a second or even a third interview if necessary, keeping in mind that a couple of two-hour interviews are far more pleasurable and productive than one four-hour interview.

7) Treat these talks as conversations rather than a formal interview. The more relaxed you keep the meeting, the more fun both you and the person you are interviewing will have.

8) Sometimes you may run into delicate situations involving relatives who don't care for each other, or some kind of unseemly information or even a scandal that a relative does not want to discuss. These situations must be treated carefully and with a good deal of common sense. If you need to find out information about, for instance, a deceased uncle of yours, and the person you are interviewing did not like this uncle and doesn't want to discuss him, then try to find someone else who will talk about your uncle rather than pressuring someone who never got along with him. Likewise, if a relative does not want to discuss a scandalous incident in the family history, find another relative who was not connected to the scandal but who knows the details to pass on the information to you. Tact and diplomacy will further your quest to find your family roots.

9) When it comes time to transpose the tape, don't feel as though you have to get every spoken word. In some instances—particularly for information that you don't feel is crucial at this stage of your research—you may want to simply jot a few words about the subject being discussed along with the point in the tape where is occurs.

INTERVIEWING FAMILY MEMBERS BY MAIL

At times it is difficult to arrange a live interview with a relative because of money and geographical considerations, so you may choose to interview a relative by mail. It is a good idea to have a cover letter (*see Figure 4*) for your questionnaire.

Figure 4

Dear Aunt Violet,

As you may have heard, I have been tracing our family roots in the hopes of putting together a complete history of our family. So far it has been a tremendously exciting challenge, made much easier by all of the help I have received from my relatives, both close and distant, who have provided me with a wide variety of facts and stories.

I would be extremely grateful if you could also offer your help. I have sent along a family group chart, and I would appreciate it if you would take the time to fill it out as best you can. I have also sent along a few questions for you to answer, and would be thankful if you could answer these for me too.

When I am finished with this project, I plan on making copies for everyone in the family, and I'll be sure that you are one of the first to receive it.

Best wishes,

(your name)

PS—If you have any family records (diaries, bibles, photos, birth and death certificates, etc.) that you could possibly send me so that I may make a photocopy of them, I would be eternally grateful. Or, if you would like to make a photocopy for me, I would be more than happy to reimburse you for the cost.

Along with your letter, include a brief questionnaire, with direct, to-the-point questions. Keep the number of questions you ask to a reasonable amount, or else you might discourage your potential source. You should also leave enough space after each question for relatives to write in their answers and include a blank family group chart. Finally, include a self-addressed, stamped envelope for their convenience.

You may also find yourself writing to a relative whom you have never met, or even to someone who does not know that the two of you are related. In this instance, a cover letter that provides background on you and how you are related to the person to whom you are writing will be necessary. Here is a sample opening paragraph; the remainder of the letter should be similar to the one included above:

Dear Mr. Smith,

My name is Jordan Jones, and I am your third cousin once removed. While we have never met, you may have heard about me through your grandfather, who still keeps in touch with my father. You and I are related because your great-great-grandfather, Rick Jones, was the brother of my great-grandfather, Steve Jones. I realize this can be confusing, so I have included a chart that will help you understand these intricate relationships.

I have recently become interested in tracing my family roots. . . .

Finding Relics in the Attic and Basement

When visiting or interviewing an older relative, ask if you may look at any family records he or she may have saved. If possible, try to gain access to the attics and/or cellar, where things from the past are often stored. We can almost guarantee that such searches will provide you with a storehouse of information. It's also a good idea to carry along a magnifying glass in order to make out old and faded handwriting. Here is what to look for:

Family Bibles—Early American tradition stipulated that all vital family information be written inside the family bible, often on the inside of the front cover or the first one or two pages. Bibles from the nineteenth century often printed inner pages delegated only to birth, marriage, and death records. When viewing this information, always compare the publication date of the bible with the date of entry or date of birth of the person who recorded the information. This way, you'll be able to tell whether the material was entered after the fact, or if it is indeed first-hand information. You should also look carefully at the handwriting: if it is uniform throughout, then chances are good that one person entered the information in one setting, from memory or second and third-hand information, long after the actual births and deaths of the parties involved. If the handwriting differs from entry to entry, and the older entries are more faded than recent entries, then you most likely have a much more authentic family record, as different family members entered in events as they actually occurred.

Diaries—While these will rarely provide you with hard facts, they will give you a unique insight into the cultural and intellectual history of a certain period of time. It should also be noted that many diaries from colonial times have been published. They may be of use to you if you are fortunate enough to trace your family roots to the dawning of our country. For instance, Judge Samuel Sewall's Diary covers the Boston area from 1674 to 1729, and Joshua Hempstead's diary offers a great deal of information about New London, Connecticut, from 1711 to 1748.

Books—Within their covers, books can offer a surprising fountain of information. If you look carefully, you may find old letters, newspaper clippings, underlined passages, a bookplate with names and addresses, and other possibly revealing information.

Letters—A valuable source, not only for the details of your family's history that may be contained within the letters themselves, but for what's on the outside of the envelope: addresses, return addresses, postmarks, and dates.

Family records—Wills, deeds, birth and death certificates, passports, armed forces papers, college diplomas, contracts, professional certificates, church records, health papers, yearbooks, deeds . . .

if it's a legal document of any kind, it most likely contains information you can use.

Samplers and quilts—Sometimes seamstresses who created these fabric art pieces often stitched in names and date. Examine them closely!

Miscellaneous items—Silverware, tea pots, jewelry, watches . . . almost anything that can contain an inscription should be sought. At the very least, ask the relative who owns the item for an explanation, for he or she might subsequently reveal key information.

In *Leaving Cold Sassy*, Katrina Kenison described how Olive Ann Burns took notes during discussions with her ailing mother about their family history. The long afternoons drew them close, diverting attention from pain and illness. By the time her mother died, Olive Ann had also interviewed aging aunts and uncles, siblings, and cousins. She found love letters her parents had written during World War I, grocery bills dating from the Great Depression, report cards, telegrams, early photographs, letters, and anecdotes contributed by other relatives—even a floor plan of the family house. "What hooked me on family history was not the names and dates," Burns said, "it was the handed-down stories that bring the dead back to life." Her project turned into *Leaving Cold Sassy*, a novel set in turn-of-the-century Georgia, and brought to life a sumptuous story of humor and the appreciation of eccentricity.

So, talk with relatives, rummage through those old boxes, you never know. . . .

Chapter Five

USING COMPUTERS FOR GENEALOGICAL SEARCHES

𝒯he impact of computers on genealogical searches has been phenomenal. No, you can't find everything you need on a computer to complete your family tree. But, in the not distant future, you will find more than you ever expected.

Once on-line, you can use the Internet to view library card catalogs, visit search databases, access the e-mail or phone numbers of people across the world through search directories (such as *Netscape Whitepages*— www. Netscape. com/netcenter/whitepages.html—similar to the directories provided by your telephone company), post questions on bulletin boards for others to answer, purchase supplies, download genealogy software demonstrations to try out before buying-the list of possibilities increases each day! Those interested in these technological advances might want to read the bimonthly *The Computer Genealogist* (101 Newbury Street, Boston, MA 02116, nehgs@nehgs.org), which is published by the New England Historical Genealogy Society.

INTERNET SEARCHES

The most popular way to access the Internet is to use your own or somebody else's computer (e.g., a friend, at the library) with a modem (a built-in component that allows your computer to "talk" to other computers through phone lines or alternate technology). Computer companies continue to upgrade their models, so your computer should ideally be three years old or less to take advantage of software programs and to have the necessary speed. Next, you need an Internet on-line service provider. In the past, America Online and CompuServe dominated the field; now, a host of others have joined the competition. Once you have made the choice, you will either download their software from their Internet site or install the software they provide on disk. To use these services, connect your phone jack with a cable to your computer and dial in to their private network.

Another way you can access the Internet is to use your television as a monitor and buy an Internet keyboard access device that can connect with your phone line. The cost per month for service is about the same as commercial computer online services. (Telephone companies recently began offering Internet access using wireless phones. The phones feature microbrowser capabilities and older phones can be upgraded to provide the same features. At this point, these Web-enabled phones only offer text-based versions of web sites.)

E-MAIL, MAILING LISTS, AND NEWSGROUPS

Electronic mail (or "e-mail") allows users to send messages at any time of the day or night and to as many people as you want. You can also attach computer files. Because some services can't handle bulky e-mail, be considerate and keep messages short. Have on file a written, ready-to-use query for each person or surname that you are researching to save time and effort when launching new correspondences.

E-mail also allows you to participate in group discussions known as mailing lists and news groups that sort messages by specific topics. You can read and post messages in these ongoing conversations that are good for posting genealogy questions.

A mailing list is overseen by a list manager who makes sure users properly get on and off a subscription list. These lists have two e-mail addresses. One is to send commands (such as "subscribe"), the second is to send actual messages to other list subscribers. When you post your subscription message (generally just the word "subscribe") in the text body, eliminate your e-mail signature if you have one posted in the message. Extraneous words invalidate the initial subscription message.

One of the earliest and most well known of the literally hundreds of mailings lists is Roots-L. Because it has so many subscribers you may want to join a smaller group, but do see the many past messages stored on *ROOTS-L* (http://www.rootsweb.com).

To subscribe, send an e-mail message to:
ROOTS-L-request@rootsweb.com
Type this message: subscribe
and do not use your signature file if you have one

For a listing of mailing lists, consult:
Genealogy Resources on the Internet
http://members.aol.com/johnf14246/gen_mail.html

Genealogy Home
http://www.genhomepage.com

World Wide Web

Part of the Internet, the World Wide Web is a multimedia presentation of information pages that can be connected, thus resulting in a "web" of sites. This exciting advance for genealogists offers on-line searchable databases and information sites on almost anything.

For example, Ancestry (http://www.ancestry.com) has on-line the *American Genealogical-Biographics Index (AGBI)*, a collection that would fill 200 volumes if it were printed, and contains several million records along with 590 other databases (with 95 million more records). Ancestry charges a small fee for searches.

To get to these web sites, type in the Web address (Uniform Resource Locator "URL") that starts with "http://", use a search engine, or follow a link from one page to the next ("surf"). When you find a useful site, for instance, a Soundex converter for census searchers, "bookmark" it, which means you can find it again whenever you need.

The "home page" is the first screen you will see on a web site. That page characteristically lists contents that you "click" with the mouse for access. If the site has information of which you would like a permanent copy, not only can you print out the information, you also can "copy" the information and "paste" it in your word-processing document.

When using the information, be as careful about source authenticity as you would with print sources, and document the URL, page title, and date of the last web site revision. Compare with the original records if possible to verify on-line information. As you become more comfortable with the Web and accumulate enough family information, you may want to set up your own home page for others to use.

The number of genealogy web sites makes it tough to pick out a few for you to view.

One of the best to start with is by Cyndi Howells, the author of *Cyndi's List of Genealogy Sites* on the

Internet (http://www.cyndilist.com). Not only does she list individual countries and ethnic groups, she has thousands of more sites, including personal home pages. Two other good sites are *My Virtual Reference Desk* (http://refdesk.com/factgene.html) and *Searchable Genealogy Links* (http://www.bcl.com/users/sgl).

In the spring of 1999, the Mormon Church launched its web site *FamilySearch* (http://www.family-search.org) and was receiving 7 million visits a day. Your first stop on the site is the Search for Ancestors search engines. After entering names or key words, you'll soon learn what information the church has and information on the thousands of other genealogical Web sites that have linked to *FamilySearch*.

GENEALOGY SOFTWARE

Recent years have also seen a proliferation of genealogy software. You can download (transfer) files from the Internet onto your computer, or get software from software companies, genealogy mail order and on-line stores, genealogy societies, and conventions. One example is:

Family History SourceGuide
Salt Lake Distribution Center
1999 West 1700 South
Salt Lake City, UT 84104

The software references resources of the Family History Library and names local resources in each state. It includes blank forms and census worksheets.

Software also allows genealogists to store, organize, and present data. When genealogists first began using software to enter data, there wasn't a standard entry mode. Developers then created a way of exchanging genealogical data: GEDCOM (Genealogical Data Communication) allows genealogy software of all types to transfer data between programs.

You have your pick today of genealogy software programs—all with a multitude of features. If you don't have software already, take your time to get the one right for you. Don't waste too much time entering data on a software program that you may ultimately abandon. So, when picking software, remember to make sure it is GEDCOM compatible. You may also want your program to store video and audio recordings, have space for notes, print attractively, link to the Internet, allow the effortless creation of a Web page, or make changes easily. Some database programs have been revised several times to be state-of-the art and include a CD-ROM bundle with popular indexes, such as:

Generations Family Tree Grande Suite
Sierra On-Line 3380 - 146th Place SE
Bellevue, WA 98007, 10800-757-7707
http://www.sierra.com

Family TreeMaker
Broderbund Software
39500 Stevenson Place
Fremont, CA 94539
http://www.familytreemaker.com

Ancestors and Descendants
Adventures in Ancestry
10714 Hepburn Circle
Culver City, CA 90232-3717
800-237-5333
http://www.aia-and.com/

Personal Ancestral File
Salt Lake Distribution Center
1999 W. 1700 South
Salt Lake City, UT 84014-4233
800-537-5950
Developed by The Church of Jesus Christ of
Latter-Day Saint for its members.

Most programs can pull from their databases family charts of all types. Expect your program to make ancestor, descendant, pedigree, Family group, and Ahnentafel reports. Some can even take a database record and present it in text form; however, page after page of the same style text gets wearisome quick!

Genelines (Progeny Software, Box 1600, 232 Main Street, Wolfville, NS BOP Ixo, Canada, 10800-565-0018, www.progenysoftware.com) has the capability to place your family in context of other historical events. It works with popular genealogical software to show life events for individuals and can trace family members over time showing when different family members were alive.

Chapter Six

THE TREMENDOUS RICHES OF LIBRARIES

TAKE ADVANTAGE OF YOUR LOCAL LIBRARY

*Y*ou've talked with living family members and gone through your closets looking for anything that may hold a clue to your roots. "What's next," you might ask. Well, now it's time to begin searching through the wealth of *published* genealogical material at your disposal.

Genealogical material can be found in books, genealogical magazines, local histories, genealogical and historical society publications, and in publications by non-genealogical organizations, clubs, and even schools. The entry to this mass of information is to establish the family line you are researching first, and in which area of the country your search begins. With these basic facts, you are ready to take advantage of library riches.

Start with your local library and the library in the area where your family lived. Even the smallest libraries should have copies of town newspapers and local histories. Many libraries and library systems have their catalogs on-line and you can search their holdings from your computer. Be aware that the catalog may be limited and not yet list its entire holdings on-line.

Ideally, the state in which your search begins has a state library system (that contains all its individual public libraries' holdings on-line) and a state historical library. Smaller libraries within each state, too, have genealogical collections that may be indexed on the state library system. See the web sites of the state system for an on-line holdings listing.

Most libraries use the "Interlibrary Loan System." University, public, and private libraries belong to this consortium of institutions, and through it you can borrow books from libraries across the country. To make things even easier, the waiting period to receive books through the Interlibrary Loan System is usually only a week or two.

If your local library is not a member of the Interlibrary Loan System, visit other libraries with genealogical collections. The appendix contains listings of libraries whose collections include an impressive genealogical section. You may also want to use the World Wide Web to find libraries, such as the site *Directory of Genealogical Libraries in the United States* (http://www.greenheart.com/rdietz/gen_libs.htm) or *Libraries and Archives Resources* (http:// www.dcn.davis. ca.us/~vctinney/archives.htm).

WHAT TO ASK LIBRARIANS

Ideally, you can visit each library to view books on the county and local area as well as histories on local churches, schools, and organizations. If that is not possible, try contacting librarians by mail, phone, or e-mail. Take note that researching genealogical research requests from individuals outside the librarians' lending area is on the bottom of their list of things-to-do. Letters that begin with "Would you please send me everything you have on the following individual and family" will probably go unanswered. However, requesting information on any books about the family in question may prove far more fruitful. Include a request to pass on your questions to the local genealogical or historical society if the library staff is unable to perform the research for you. If your request is not acknowledged, write directly to the local genealogical and historical society.

LIBRARIES OF SPECIAL GENEALOGICAL SIGNIFICANCE

THE LIBRARY OF THE CHURCH OF JESUS CHRIST OF LATTER-DAY SAINTS (LDS)

Not only is this the largest genealogical library in the world, it also makes its collection available through 3,200 Family History Centers across the U.S. and around the world. For more than one hundred years, the church has sent missionaries to gather genealogical records throughout the world and spends millions every year microfilming records on site. Record originals are stored in a granite vault in the Wasatch Mountains 25 miles southeast of Salt Lake. The Mormon Church encourages its members to trace their ancestors so they can offer departed relatives the opportunity to embrace the Mormon faith in life after death.

With its extensive genealogical studies, there is a good chance that the records of your relatives, whether or not they follow the Mormon faith, are contained within this massive library. A vast part of The Family History Library's collection is on microfilm that may be lent to patrons for a small fee.

The library itself is at 35 N West Temple, Salt Lake City, UT 84150. Their phone number is 801-240-2331, and helpful staff there can guide your search. To find a local Family History Center, call (800) 346-6044, or look under the white pages of your telephone directory under "Church of Jesus Christ of LDS," or see

Family History Library (http://lds.org/en/main.html) in the section "family history resources."

LIBRARY OF CONGRESS

Although you have to actually go to the Library of Congress to use its collection, the effort is worthwhile for serious genealogists. It has one of the world's best collections of genealogy information (both national and international) and an extensive local history collection (more than 100,000 local histories). Access the Library's catalog through its web site (http://lcweb.loc.gov/rr/genealogy/lhg.html) to identify holdings. Or you may want to read James Neagles' *The Library of Congress: A Guide to Genealogical and Historical Research* (Ancestry, 1990), an extensive guide to the library's genealogical collection that includes maps. The Library also offers free guides to its collection. You can write or visit the library at:

> Local History and Genealogy Reading Room
> Jefferson Building
> 10 First Street, SE
> Washington, DC 20540

OTHER SPECIAL LIBRARIES

Dozens of libraries are famous for their genealogical collections. These genealogical meccas include New York Public Library, the Los Angeles Public Library, and National Library of Canada. For instance, the second-largest genealogy library in the United States is Allen

County Public Library, Fort Wayne, Indiana. It has more than half a million books, manuscripts, microfilms, and microfiches. A thousand more items are added to the collection each month. The library holds the distinction of having the largest English language genealogy and local history periodical collection with more than 3,000 annual subscriptions. The microtext collection emphasizes Connecticut, Illinois, Indiana, Kentucky, Massachusetts, New York, North Carolina, Ohio, Pennsylvania, South Carolina, Tennessee, Vermont, and West Virginia. They can be reached at:

Allen County Library
P. O. Box 2270
900 Webster Street
Fort Wayne, IN 46801-2270
219-421-1225
http://www.acpl.lib.in.us/

Smaller libraries, too, often concentrate on genealogical topics, such as the American Genealogical Lending Library (P. O. Box 244, Bountiful, UT 84011) and those libraries contained within museums or belonging to local historical and genealogical societies. Examples of these collections are:

American Antiquarian Society
185 Salisbury Street
Worcester, MA 01609
508-755-5221
http://www.americanantiquarian.org

This private library has more than seventeen thousand genealogies, sixty thousand local histories, and one of the largest collections of printed material relating to the first 250 years of the United States.

Genealogical Center Library
P. O. Box 71343
Marietta, GA 30007-1343

For a small membership fee, you receive a copy of the catalog and can borrow some of its thousands of genealogical books and quarterlies for two weeks.

Specific information libraries can also be gold mines, especially for those who need to prove a familial relationship with a war ancestor for an association membership. These libraries can provide not only carefully documented genealogies, but are also often stocked with valuable reference sources.

Confederate Research Center
Harold B. Simpson Hill College History Complex
112 Lamar Drive
Box 619
Hillsboro, TX 76645-0619
http://hillcollege.hill-college.cc.tx.us/crc/crc.htm

Continental Society Daughters of Indian Wars
(1607–1900)
(Library housed in McElreath Library in the Atlanta Historical Center, see Appendix)

Daughters of the American Revolution Museum
Library
300 Alamo Plaza
Box 1401
San Antonio, TX 78295-1401
210-225-1071

National Society Daughters of the American
Revolution Library
1776 D. Street, N. W.
Washington, DC 200006-5303
202-879-3229
http://www.dar.org

National Society of the Sons of the American
Revolution Library
1000 South Fourth Street
Louisville, KY 40203

When investigating libraries, take note that organizations your ancestors belonged to may have their own records. The Elks, Freemasons, Knights of Columbus, Grange, Rotary, Kiwanis, and Lions fraternal organizations hold files on members dating back to the association founders. Typically, these files have only lodge initiation dates and member death dates, although the site of a local lodge may turn up more information as web sites, such as *The Independent Order of Odd Fellows* (http://www.ioof. org) that offers information on past and present members, or you can write the I.O.O.F. at Sovereign Grand Lodge, 422 North Trade Street, Winston-Salem, NC 27101-2830. Also, look to your relatives' schools and colleges, which retain student enrollment records, yearbooks, and rosters that offer ancestral information.

WHAT YOU CAN FIND IN LIBRARIES

PUBLISHED GENEALOGIES

Always investigate to see whether someone else has done the research you plan to do. The local library where your family has lived is a good bet for a published genealogy of your relatives. These published works range from a hand-written photocopy to a bound volume with gold-embossed lettering. However, the work will be there only if someone donated it, so chances are dicey whether you will find one or not. But it's worth your time to find out!

Now, many libraries have published genealogies useful in your research. Some may prove helpful for a description of the times, while others may actually contain information on your family members. One way to find these genealogies is to use the many indexes of printed genealogies. They will let you know if the genealogy of the family you are searching for has been published in either periodical or book form. You simply look up the family name—making certain you check variant spellings—to find any genealogies published on that name, including publication date, publisher name, and other details. There is no one index to all genealogies, so, if necessary, search through a variety of indexes.

Once you find a reference to a published genealogy, you have three options: first, you can search for a copy of the genealogy in the library where you found the reference in the index; second, you can contact the publisher that specializes in printed genealogies and supplies (see Appendix) and purchase the book; and third, you can contact other libraries to see whether they have it in their collections.

If you are fortunate enough to find a copy of a genealogy of a family in which you are interested, and go on to discover that it indeed contains your line of descent, copy the information you need and create an ancestral chart. When working on the chart, write down the page number where you find the information on each name you are jotting down. That way, if you ever need to go back for a fact, you won't have to search through pages and pages to find the information.

A word of caution: Just because you find a beautifully bound volume containing the genealogy of one of your descent lines, this does not guarantee that the information is accurate. For all you know, the person who compiled the genealogy could have based it on hearsay, inaccurate memories, and then printed it and bound the work in a gold-embossed leather cover to look professional. Many times, in fact, a few scraps of faded paper can contain a genealogy much more accurate than one that has been printed and bound. The lesson here is never take any prepublished genealogy as gospel; always compare dates, facts, and relationships against either the original or some type of official records.

GENEALOGICAL PERIODICALS

Genealogical journals and newsletters have been published throughout the history of the United States, which means you have a huge amount of published material from which to sort. More than a thousand magazines publish information on societies and genealogical libraries. Some even invite you to write in with questions, in the hope that other readers may help you in your information search.

Besides the many regional and state genealogical periodicals, there are general periodicals pertaining to genealogy that offer current topics, top-notch research techniques, advertisements, and means for genealogists to contact each other. A few are:

Ancestry Magazine
Ancestry, Inc.
P. O. Box 990
Orem, UT 84059-0990
http://www.ancestry.com

Everton's Genealogical Helper
P. O. Box 368
Logan, UT 84321
http://www.everton.com/

Genealogical Journal
P. O. Box 1144
Salt Lake City, UT 84110
http://www.infouga.org/journal.htm

Heritage Quest
P. O. Box 329
Bountiful, UT 84011-0329
http://www.heritagequest.com/

Fortunately a good number of indexes to these publications exist to help you find a piece of information about one of your ancestors. A shortcut is the Periodical Source Index (PERSI), both in a multi-volume print or CD-ROM format, compiled by the Allen County Library. (It is available for sale from Ancestry, see address above.) It is a subject index to more than 5,000 genealogy and local history periodicals written in English and French since 1800 with some information pre-1800. Articles are indexed according to locality, family surname, and/or research method.

Also, try out UnCover (http://uncweb.carl.org/dev/howto.html), a one-stop shopping place for more than 18,000 journals and magazines dating from 1989 to the present. The good news is that UnCover has more than 200 genealogical publications (and adding more!), and the article you order can be delivered within 48 hours (in one hour if you use the express service) by FAX, Monday through Friday.

Increasingly, UnCover is offering articles that can also be delivered directly to a personal computer in its Desktop Image Delivery service. For articles earlier than 1989, if you have the complete citation (author, article title, periodical title and issue number, page numbers, etc.), UnCover can find and deliver those, too.

LOCAL HISTORIES

Most towns, cities, and counties have published local histories about their founding and historical events. A great many of these local histories were written at the end of the nineteenth century when commercial publishers packaged information with subscriptions from businesses and people willing to pay to be included in the history. Often, it was a situation where the bigger the payment, the larger the entry. Also, when cities and towns celebrated landmark anniversaries, town histories were also produced. Often, these entries contain information about other family members and their original homeland. Don't overlook these books if your ancestor isn't listed. They may have clues, such as the country where the majority of the settlers originated from or historical details that you can use when you ultimately sit down to write a family history.

DIRECTORIES

Although larger libraries have the most offerings in terms of directories, you may be surprised at the holdings of a local library. City directories, which date back to the 1700s for larger cities, began as business directories, then later added all residents. Most list a person's address and occupation in a particular city, and some even list former residences. Genealogists can use directories to better find relatives in censuses, learn how long a family resided in a certain location, discover deaths (e.g., a woman listed as with her husband one year, and then as a widow the next year), and the size of a family. Other directories to look out for are statewide gazetteers, livestock brand registrations, telephone directories, and professional directories (e.g., a listing of dentists in a particular state).

Primary Source Media (http://www.citydirectories. psmedia.com/abstract.htm) recently produced a full-test searchable archive of U.S. city directories starting in 1859 with a concentration on the major port and transit hub cities. The entries are reproduced on original page facsimiles. With this on-line resource you can search any word or phrase across several directories simultaneously. The company plans to add directories from the United Kingdom and Scotland in the near future.

Newspapers

Newspapers have existed in the United States since the country's origin. Searching through newspaper microfilms can be a chore, true, but so worth it when you find an ancestor's obituary, marriage record, or news article. You also get a flavor of the times that makes you experience history in a whole new way. Usually, the most efficient way to use newspapers is to know the date for which you are searching information, and look at the news editions on that date and around that date. Some papers are indexed, and you can find information on, say, a business your relative owned or worked at by using the index.

Genealogical Publishers and Booksellers

Whether you locate a particular publication in one of the indexes mentioned above, or if you simply want to inquire about published material on a certain region of the country, the genealogical publishers and book sellers listed below should be able to help you. Write to them requesting either their catalog (usually free) or information on a particular publication in which you are interested.

Ancestry.com, Inc.
P. O. Box 990
Orem, UT 84059
801-426-3500
http://www.ancestry.com

Appleton's Online
800-777-3601
http://www.appletons.com/genealogy/homepage.html

Barnette's Family Tree
1001 West Loop North
Houston, TX 77004
713-684-4633
http://www.barnettsbooks.com/

Boyd Publishing Company
P. O. Box 367
Milledgeville, GA 31061
http://www.home.net/~gac/index.html
Frontier Press
http://www.frontierpress.com/frontier.cgi

Genealogical Publishing Company
1001 N. Calvert Street
Baltimore, MD 21202
800-296-6687
http://www.genealogybookshop.com/
genealogybookshop/index.html

Genealogy Bookstore.com
http://www.genealogybookstore.com/

Genealogy Unlimited
P. O. Box 537
Orem, UT 84059
800-666-4363

Global Genealogy
13 Charles Street, Suite 102
Milton, Ontario, Canada L9T 2G5
800-361-5168
http://www.globalgenealogy.com/ordrmain.htm

Hearthstone Bookshop
http://www.hearthstonebooks.com/

Heritage Book News
1540-E Pointer Ridge Place
Bowie, Maryland 20716
800-398-7709
http://www.heritagebooks.com

Higginson Book Company
148 Washington Street
P.O. Box 778
Salem, MA 01970
http://www.higginsonbooks.com/

Origins
4327 Milton Avenue
Janesville, WI 53546
608-757-2777
http://www.angelfire.com/biz/origins1/

Picton Press
P. O. Box 250
Rockport, ME 04865
207-236-6565

TCI Genealogical Resources
P. O. Box 1312
Highland, CA 92346
http://www.tcigenealogy,com/

The Genealogy Store
http://www.genservices.com/store/index.htm

Willow Bend Books
800-876-6103
http://www.willowbend.net/default.asp

Windmill Publications
6628 Uebelhack Road
Mt. Vernon, IN 47620
812-985-9214

Ye Olde Genealogie Shoppe
P. O. Box 39128
Indianapolis, IN 46239
800-419-0200
http://www.yogs.com/

GENEALOGICAL SOCIETIES

Genealogical societies not only offer classes, con-
ferences, and research tours, they also typically publish
periodicals. Your local society often will focus more

on meetings and publish a newsletter, while national societies produce high-quality publications with genealogy articles and research strategies. The National Genealogical Society publishes the *NGS Newsletter*, *NGS Computer Interest Group Digest*, and the *NGS Quarterly*. It also has a 30,000 volume library for member use.

> National Genealogical Society
> 4527 seventeenth Street North
> Arlington, VA 22207-2399
> 1-800-473-0060
> ngs@ngsgenealogy.org
> http://www.ngsgenealogy.org

Other societies can be found by contacting:

Federation of Genealogical Societies
P. O. Box 200940
Austin, TX 78720-0940
1-888-FGS-1500
www.fgs.org
fgs-office@fgs.org

Chapter Seven

CHURCH RECORDS AND CEMETERIES

WESTERN CIVILIZATION'S RECORD KEEPERS

The Church is one of the oldest organized institutions in Western civilization. Before Reformation in Europe, the clergy, who studied religious works, were the only people who could read and write. As such, the duty to keep state records fell to them, as kings were eager to have accurate records of the citizenry so that no one could escape paying taxes!

The result of this has been records kept by religious organizations for almost a thousand years. If you are thinking this seems too good to be true, you're right. In many cases their accuracy is in question, and in Europe, where the church and the state acted as one body, corruption undoubtedly tainted records at times. Also, natural disasters and warfare have destroyed innumerable records. Imagine how many records were lost in Europe because of the World War II bombing raids! In America, where the church has always been forced away from state affairs, meticulous record-keeping was not seen as a duty of the clergy.

Don't lose heart. Even though church records were lost, many exist today. Some contain information that cannot be found anywhere else, and some contain facts that corroborate information in other records. These church records can help, in particular, locate birth, marriage, and death information. They do vary among denominations: Quaker, Dutch reformed, Anglican, Catholic, and other European churches traditionally maintained logs of births, marriages, and deaths; Baptist, United Brethren, and other America-born religions recorded little more than membership rosters.

HOW TO USE CHURCH RECORDS

To use church records effectively, remember two trends in American religious history. First, when Europeans initially came to this continent and formed colonies, they distrusted the church entering their affairs so much that religious wedding ceremonies were outlawed. Weddings were considered civil affairs, and as a result, civil magistrates performed them. Therefore, if you find mention of a wedding in a church record that dates back to the colonies, take a closer look. The record is probably not of a wedding but of a marriage bann, or an intention to marry, and there is no guarantee that such a marriage ever took place. If you assume that such a bann was fulfilled, you might start researching the wrong family by mistake if the two never actually married. A second fact to be aware of is that religious groups in America actively campaigned for new members. As a result, people often converted from one faith to another. When a person converted, their name was often dropped from church records.

How do find what faith your family members were? A good start is to know their European homeland. If they were German or Dutch, chances are they were either Dutch Reformed, Lutheran, or Catholic. If they were from Italy or certain parts of Ireland, they were Catholic. And if they were from Scotland or Ireland, they were probably Presbyterian. Knowing this, you can compare that with the colony in which they settled. Catholics, for instance tended to settle in Maryland, while Presbyterians preferred Virginia.

The singlemost problem with church records from this country is that they are rarely complete. Ministers and priests usually had to maintain records by themselves, and they were notoriously bad at doing so. Even worse, when a priest actually did keep accurate records, he sometimes took them with him when he moved, instead of leaving them for his successor. Nevertheless, don't forget to check for the existence of church records about your ancestors.

When reading church records, keep in mind that if only one parent was a member of a church, then only his or her name may be listed on membership rosters. This is also true for the children of a married couple who did not always join the same church as their parents, and thus would not be included in their parents' church records. The easiest way to determine how many family members attended the same church is to find the baptismal records of a child; such records will most likely list the names of the parents present at the ceremony. If only one parent was present, then the other probably did not belong to the same church. However, if you find the baptismal records for several children, and sometimes both parents are listed as attending and sometimes only one, then this indicates that both parents were members of the same church, but one was simply not able to attend all the ceremonies.

When going through the baptismal records for a family with several children, you might notice a change in one of the parents' names. This means that, regrettably, a parent probably died and the other remarried shortly thereafter. Correctly note the parents of the ancestor you are researching; if, for example, you do not notice a change in the name of the father between the first and second children, then you will trace the wrong family line.

Another church record, *Records of Admittance*, not only specifically states which family members joined a particular church, it can also indicate the family member's former church and former faith.

HOW TO OBTAIN CHURCH RECORDS

To access church records, either visit the church if it is still in operation, or write to the church directly.

If the church records you want are from a defunct church, write either the local historical society or to the archives of the particular denomination in which you are interested. If your family member was a member of the clergy, the archives may contain a biography on the family member and news clippings. Here, for instance, are some churches that keep archives:

American Baptist Historical Society
1106 South Goodman Street
Rochester, NY 14620

American Catholic Historical Society
P. O. Box 84
Philadelphia, PA 19105

American Congregational Association
Congregational Library
14 Beacon Street
Boston, MA 02108

American Jewish Archives
3101 Clifton Avenue
Cincinnati, OH 45220-2488
513-221-1875
http://server.huc.edu/aja/

Archives of the Greek Orthodox
Arch-Diocese of North America
10 East 79th Street
New York, NY 10021

Archives of the Moravian Church
41 West Locust Street
Bethlehem PA 18018

Archives of the Mother Church
The First Church of Christ Scientist
107 Falmouth Street
Boston, MA 02110

Lutheran Historical Society
Lutheran Theological Seminary
Wentz Library
Gettysburg, PA 17325

Mennonite Historical Library
565 Yoder Rd.
Box 82
Harleysville, PA 19438
215-256-3020

Mennonite Library & Archives
Bethel College
300 E. 27th Street
North Newton, KS 67117

Methodist Historical Center
326 New Street
Philadelphia, PA 19106

Presbyterian Church Department History
P. O. Box 849
Montreat, NC 28757

Protestant Episcopal Church
Church Historical Society
P. O. Box 2247
606 Rathervue Place
Austin, TX 78768

Society of Evangelical and Reformed Church
Archives
College Avenue and James Street
Lancaster, PA 17604

Many church records can also be found at local and
state archives and libraries.

CEMETERIES

If you think about it, cemeteries are genealogies written in stone! If you already know the birth and death dates
of your ancestors, go to the cemeteries in which they are
buried anyway. Not only will you confirm your records,
you may also get a feel for the person from the inscription
and the type of tombstone. You may also discover relatives
you never knew of, so look at as many tombstones as possible as relatives may not be buried together.

But what if you don't know in which cemetery your
ancestor is buried? That's a bit trickier. It helps if you
know the person's religion, because Catholics and Jews
usually have a separate cemetery from the town cemetery. Also, a local church often has its own cemetery
and if your relative was a member, that person may be
in the church cemetery. Churches that have their own
cemeteries can tell you not only whether the person is
there, but exactly where that person is buried.

If you know the funeral home used for the burial,
you can contact it for confirmation and location of
your relative's grave. The grave may or may not have a
tombstone, because tombstones were expensive and

not everyone had one. Also, the tombstone may have deteriorated through time or been vandalized.

The local funeral home records will also list the date and place of death, spouse's name, birth place, itemized list of funeral and burial expenses, and a copy of the person's obituary that can save you a search through newspapers. If you still are coming up short, you may find a local index of cemeteries that lists the people buried in a particular cemetery. They can often be found at local libraries. Often, there are smaller, rural cemeteries besides the town cemetery where a person is buried. For instance, a farmer who lived five miles north of town may be buried in the cemetery close to his farm rather than the town cemetery. In some instances, an ancestor is buried in a private graveyard that may no longer have any markers. If that is true, talk to older citizens and family members to see what they remember.

Recording Tombstone Information

Tombstones are made of varying stone grades, some of which were soft and have deteriorated through time. If the writing on these stones is illegible, don't assume anything. Also, don't change anything. For example, if the stone reads, "Jane, consort of John Niedens," don't replace consort with wife. "Consort" means that her husband was alive at the time of her death, but "wife" can mean that he was either dead or alive. Write down the inscription, then rub chalk over the gravestone so the letters read easily. Next, photograph the tombstone. Third, make a rubbing of the headstone. Place a piece of wax paper over the tombstone, and rub the paper with a crayon or soft pencil to reveal some information that may have been hard to read. If still indecipherable, place brackets around questionable words (e.g., [consort]). This way you can remember which part was taken from the stone, and which you deduced through other information. The date and place of death are generally accurate, but birth dates may be inaccurate. Also, maiden names for women are not usually recorded.

Cemeteries bring back the past, and no genealogical search is truly complete without them.

Chapter Eight

LOCAL AND STATE RECORDS

A WORD ABOUT PRIMARY SOURCES

*I*n research, there are basically two types of sources: primary and secondary. Primary sources (those records made during the time of the person, e.g., a family Bible, letters, journals, public records) rate higher for authenticity than secondary sources (information obtained from primary sources, e.g., newspaper articles, books) because the information provided has had less chance to be garbled, polluted, forgotten, or otherwise distorted.

Primary information sources not only give you the information you seek (such as a birth date), but almost always provide you with additional information. For example, a birth certificate will not only mention the birth date of an ancestor, but will also indicate the name of the ancestor's parents.

So far, we have discussed church records as a primary source. The next source of primary information to explore are local and state records. These documents can be categorized into two sections: Criminal and civil. Criminal records will most likely not be of use during your search. However, civil records contain vital statistics, probate, and land records, and will be found in the courthouses in the areas where your ancestors lived. In many parts of the northeast, however, they are often filed in the State Archival Depository.

RESEARCHING PRIMARY SOURCE RECORDS

While expensive in time and financial cost, traveling in person to various courthouses is the only way to ensure a thorough record search. You also might inadvertently stumble across information, such as the names of other relatives who lived in the area, that can fill in genealogy gaps. Before you visit, call ahead to find out when the courthouse is open to the public and whether it has a list of the records, (e.g., military discharge papers, polling lists, professional licenses, affidavits) that are available to the public.

The alternative is to write to the person responsible for supervising civil records known as the "clerk of the court" or the "recorder of deeds." This person, busy already with daily duties, probably gets many genealogical requests and may find it difficult to respond to your inquiry.

To increase your chances for a helpful response:

1) Be specific. Give the exact name of the ancestor for whom you are searching (including variant spellings), the exact type of record you need, and an estimate as to when the record was filed.

2) Be brief. Make the search as easy as possible. Always include a self-addressed, stamped envelope for the response, and offer to pay any costs incurred by the clerk's search.

3) If possible, ask for a photocopy of the document. Otherwise, request that all pertinent information in the records, such as dates and witnesses, be supplied.

FIRST STEPS

Think about when and where your ancestor may have done something to be entered into civil records, such as dockets, court orders, birth certificates, marriage licenses and records, leases, deeds, or wills.

Most courthouses have a surname index that will direct you to any books containing records with your ancestor's surname. Each book, in turn, is ordered by date, further simplifying your search. If, for example, you want to find the birth certificate of an ancestor named "Becker," and you know he was born sometime between 1860 and 1875, then simply search through the books that include the name "Becker" and cover that 15-year time period. If the courthouse does not have a surname index, each record book should have an index within its pages. This requires you to look through the indexes of every record book covering a certain period.

VITAL DOCUMENTS

Vital events documents record births, deaths, and marriages. Such documents have been kept with varying degrees of accuracy since the first town formed in the United States, but were not required by federal law until as late as the beginning of this century. As a result, records for a person who either was born or died in the twentieth century are fairly easy to find-simply write to the proper state office of vital records. A state-by-state list has been included in the appendix of this book to help you in your search for vital documents or see the web site *Vital Records Information for United States* (http://vitalrec.com/index.html) for contact information. For records on those U.S. citizens born outside the United States, contact the Passport Service (1111 nineteenth Street NW, Washington, DC 20522-1705).

You may want to get the very inexpensive guide (it was $2.50 in 2000; price includes shipping) from the federal government that tells you the cost of obtaining the vital record you need. Call 1-888-293-6498 or write:

The U.S. Government Printing Office
Superintendent of Documents
P. O. Box 371954
Pittsburgh, PA 15250-7954

For records pre-dating the twentieth century, you may have to do some digging, but you will probably come up with the information you need. To find the birth and death certificates of ancestors before the twentieth century, contact the local courthouse where they lived. Areas with the most inaccuracies and omission of these documents are, naturally, pioneer towns and frontier lands.

Marriage records were not standardized until recently, so these documents may be referred to as applications, bonds, certificates, consents, intentions, licenses, registers, etc. Some are records of the marriage itself, while others are merely civil versions of banns, so read carefully.

Each state differs in its record-keeping. In some states, the earliest marriage records can be found in church registers. Later records were handled by courts and counties until statewide registration was required. Besides courthouses, marriage records can be found in varying locations, including: original courts, state health or vital statistics departments, state archives, or libraries. Also look in the Records of the Bureau of Indian Affairs for Native-American marriages or Records of the Bureau of Refugees, Freedmen, and Abandoned Lands for African American marriages.

Those looking for divorce records should also look to the courthouse. The earliest divorces may be found in state records when courts and territorial or state legislatures granted divorces, separations, and petitions for feme sole (single, widowed, or divorced women) status.

When requesting any type of record copy, provide the full name of the person whose record is being requested, relevant dates, parents' names, purpose for which the copy is needed, and your relationship to the person whose record is being requested. It helps to find the record fee in advance, then send a money order for the total amount.

PROPERTY RECORDS

A large part of courthouse documents deal with the taxation, sale, and disagreement over property. While most of this property involves land, you may often find records pertaining to livestock and slave ownership. Land transactions are typically found in deed indexes. Direct indexes list by sellers (grantor) or buyers (grantees). The types of deeds you will encounter will be deeds of trust used for property transfer to pay off debts; deeds of gift used to give property, often to children; and warranty deeds that transferred property with clear title. An important land record for your purposes is the "multiple-grantor" deed, which lists all sales of a deceased landowner's property by his children. This document includes the names and birthdays of both the children and their spouses.

When studying land deeds, look to see how the property owner acquired the piece of land, since there is a good possibility that he received it from an ancestor, which will provide you with another piece of your family history puzzle. Likewise, one piece of property is often passed down from generation to generation and, as such, one deed could provide you with all the information you need to complete a particular family group chart.

Look also in land records for the name of the land owner's wife, his other relatives, where he previously lived, when he bought the land, and when he sold it.

Figure 5: GLOSSARY OF PROBATE TERMS

Abeyance: Undetermined ownership, e.g., of an unsettled estate

Abstract: A summarized document

Administrator: Person who oversees the settlement of an estate

Affidavit: Written, signed statement made under oath

Bequest: A gift made in will

Cadastral: Records, survey, or map that shows land ownership and value

Chattel: Personal property, both alive and inanimate

Consanguinity: Blood relationship

Conveyance: Record that transfers property title to one from another

Devise: To transmit property through a will

Dowager: A widow who holds property from her deceased husband

DSP: "Died sine prole," without offspring

Escheat: Property that reverts to state when there are no heirs

Guardian: Person who cares for property or minors after a death

Holographic will: A handwritten will by the person who died without help from another

Issue: Children

Kindred: Blood-related people

Legacy: Money or property received in a will

Nuncupative will: An oral will that was transcribed and witnessed by others

Primogeniture: The right of the eldest child (usually son) to inherit parents' estate

Progeny: Children

Relict: Widow and sometimes a widower

Testator: A person who died leaving a valid will

PROBATE RECORDS

Probate records (also known as estate records) are wills and testaments that deal with property. Probate records, usually in local courthouses, have existed since the dawn of civilization. Technically, the will deals primarily with an individual's personal property, while the testament is concerned with land disposal.

When an individual dies, the probate court appoints an executor to his or her will. The executor delivers the will to the court and proves its validity through the testimony of witnesses present at its signing. If the court rules the will is valid, then it is declared *testate*, and the executor distributes the land and possessions accordingly. If ruled invalid, the court declares it *intestate*, in which case an administrator is appointed to dispose of all lands and properties.

Incidentally, married women did not have the right to a will in the initial years of this country, because the court viewed married property as belonging to the husband. If the husband died and left the woman widowed, she then gained the right to a will, unless she remarried.

Genealogists value wills because they precisely document familial relationships. An individual usually bequeaths land and property to his wife, to his children (from oldest to youngest), and sometimes to distant relatives, such as grandchildren. Even when a will is declared *intestate*, the administrator must record the individual's relations.

Much like religious documents, wills allow a peek into the lives of our ancestors. You might find accurate inventories of your ancestor's possessions, allowing you to determine his or her living standard and social rank in the community. You can locate the exact plots of land your ancestor owned and even visit where they lived.

When writing to a county clerk for a copy of a last will and testament, you might only receive an "abstraction," or parts of the document, rather than the whole will itself. In such cases, ask for the following information:

1) The name of the person who wrote the will, cause of death, and place the person lived at time of death.

2) The name of all people mentioned in the will and their relationship to the deceased.

3) A list of property bequeathed

4) Names of all witnesses and executors

Along with the will, you may find accounts and settlements, petitions, sales, returns, bonds, and appointment of guardianship. You may also get a record of distribution, which indicates how the estate was divided up proportionately, the recipients, and their relationship to the deceased. Wills and testaments, also, were often disputed by relatives who felt they had been cheated out of an inheritance. These lawsuit records may often be found with an ancestor's will.

Chapter Nine

FEDERAL GOVERNMENT RESEARCH SOURCES

THE NATIONAL ARCHIVES

On the Pennsylvania Avenue side of the National Archives building in Washington, DC, an inscription reads, "The heritage of the past is the seed that brings forth the harvest of the future." Inside is indeed a harvest, and if you are able to visit the National Archives in person—something every citizen should do once in his life if only to view such grand historical documents as the Declaration of Independence, the Bill of Rights, and the Constitution, among others— a member of the staff will consult with you on search possibilities.

The best way to access records here, which include censuses, military service records, passenger ship lists, maps, and federal court cases, and others, is to go in person. If you can't, try these options:

1) Use the NARA's web site, in particular, *The Genealogy Page* (http://www.nara.gov/genealogy/). The site has a search engine for many of its records, microfilm catalogs, and a listing of genealogy workshops and publications. NARA offers free, general information leaflets on record use, military service records, and use of the Archives. To order, contact: Product Distribution NECD, National Archives, 700 Pennsylvania Avenue, NW, Washington, DC 20408, 800-234-8861.

2) Obtain a catalog of its microfilms, and rent them for a very inexpensive rate for a 30-day time period. Order the catalog from the contact information above.

3) Visit one of NARA's regional libraries. Not only do they offer much of the same information as the Washington, DC collection, they have Native American tribal claims, territorial court proceedings, migrant labor camps, weather observations, and other topics relevant to the region. Here is a list of NARA's regional libraries:

National Archives New England Region
380 Trapelo Road
Waltham, MA 02452-6399
781-647-8104
center@waltham.nara.gov
http://www.nara.gov/regional/boston.html
Area served: Maine, New Hampshire, Vermont, Massachusetts, Connecticut, and Rhode Island

National Archives Northeast Region
10 Conte Drive
Pittsfield, MA 01201-8230
413-445-6885
Pittsfield, MA 01201-8230
center@pittsfield.nara.gov
http://www.nara.gov/regional/pittsfie.html

National Archives Northeast Region
201 Varick Street
New York, NY 10014-4811
212-337-1300
archives@newyork.nara.gov
http://www.nara.gov/regional/newyork.html
Area served: New York, New Jersey, Puerto Rico, U.S. Virgin Islands

National Archives Mid-Atlantic Region
900 Market Street
Philadelphia, PA 19107-4292
215-597-3000
archives@philarch.nara.gov
http://www.nara.gov/regional/philacc.html
Area served: Delaware, Maryland, Pennsylvania, Virginia, West Virginia

National Archives Southeast Region
1557 Street Joseph Avenue
East Point, Georgia 30344-2593
404-763-7474
center@atlanta.nara.gov
http://www.nara.gov/regional/atlanta.html
*Area served: Alabama, Florida, Georgia, Kentucky,
Mississippi, North Carolina, South Carolina,
Tennessee*

National Archives Great Lakes Region
7538 South Pulaski Road
Chicago, IL 60629-5898
773-581-7816
archives@chicago.nara.gov
http://www.nara.gov/regional/chicago.html
Area served: Illinois, Minnesota, Wisconsin

National Archives Central Plains Region
2312 East Bannister Road
Kansas City, MO 64131-3011
816-926-6982
center@kansascity.nara.gov
http://www.nara.gov/regional/kansas.html
Area served: Iowa, Kansas, Missouri, Nebraska

National Archives Southwest Region
501 West Felix Street, Building 1
Fort Worth, Texas 76115-3405
817-334-5515
center@ftworth.nara.gov
http://www.nara.gov/regional/ftworth.html
Area served: Arkansas, Oklahoma, Louisiana, Texas

National Archives Rocky Mountain Region
Denver Federal Building, Building Number 48
P. O. Box 25307
Denver, Colorado 80225-0307
303-236-0804
center@denver.nara.gov
http://www.nara.gov/regional/denver.html
Area served: Colorado, Montana, New Mexico,
North Dakota, South Dakota, Utah, Wyoming

National Archives Pacific Region
24000 Avila Road (street address)
P. O. Box 6719 (mail address)
Laguna Niguel, California 92607-3497
949-360-2641
archives@laguna.nara.gov
http://www.nara.gov/regional/laguna.html
Area served: Arizona, southern California, Clark
County (Nevada)

National Archives Pacific Region
1000 Commodore Drive
San Bruno, CA 94066-2350
650-876-9001
archives@sanbruno.nara.gov
http://www.nara.gov/regional/sanfranc.html
Area served: Northern California, Guam, Hawaii,
Nevada (except Clark County), American Samoa,
Trust Territory of the Pacific Islands

National Archives Pacific Alaska Region
6125 Sand Point Way NE
Seattle, WA 98115-7999
206-526-6501
center@seattle.nara.gov
http://www.nara.gov/regional/seattle.html
Area served: Idaho, Oregon, Washington

National Archives Pacific Alaska Region
654 West Third Avenue
Anchorage, AK 99501-2145
907-271-2441
archives@alaska.nara.gov
http://www.nara.gov/regional/anchorag.html
Area served: Alaska

CENSUS RECORDS

Through census records, you can trace the migratory patterns of your ancestors, the number of people in their households, and even discover relatives by alternate name spellings. No genealogy can be considered complete until these crucial records have been studied. Although they can contain mistakes, they are an excellent way of doubling information gleaned from other sources.

The British instituted the first censuses in America during the colonial period to better tax colonists. As a result, the colonies took almost forty censuses of their populations between 1600 and 1789. In 1790, the federal government administered the first official U.S. census to gauge the country's military power in the event of war. Since then, the government has administered a new census every ten years, compiling schedules of residents within each state.

Not all United States' censuses are available to the public, because the Privacy Act of 1974 stipulated that no federal records less than 75 years old be released to the public. Another fact that you should know is that names on the census (especially the earliest) may have several spelling variants, because census takers were notoriously poor spellers and spelled phonetically. Also, people often mistrusted the census takers and did not necessarily give them accurate information. One more thing-boundaries changed as the nation aged, so the county your ancestor lived in may have a different name now, so check on this before you spend too much time reading through microfilm.

A good way to work with census is to take the most recent census and work backward, tracing your family line as far back as possible. Record all information available about your ancestors, because it may prove useful later on. Always learn about families living in the same town or county and sharing the same last name as your ancestors-you may find some relatives you never knew you had. Now for the censuses themselves, including their contents.

1790: Name of family head; free white males 16 and older; free white males under 16; free white females; slaves; and other persons, which may include workers, friends, or boarders who were not actually family members. When the British attacked Washington, DC during the War of 1812, the schedules for Delaware, Georgia, Kentucky, New Jersey, Tennessee, Virginia, and parts of

Maryland and North Carolina were burned, although many of these lost records have been restored with the help of state tax lists.

1800: Name of household head; free white males and females under the age of 10, and between the ages of 10 and 16, 16 and 26, 26 and 44, and over 44 years old.; race; and slaves. The schedules for Georgia, Indian Territory, Kentucky, Mississippi Territory, New Jersey, Northwest Territory Ohio River, Tennessee, and Virginia are entirely missing. Maine, Maryland, Massachusetts, New Hampshire, Pennsylvania, and South Carolina schedules are partially missing.

1810: Listing the same information as the previous census, this census lacks the schedules for District of Columbia, Georgia, Indiana Territory, Louisiana, Michigan, Mississippi, New Jersey, and Ohio. Those for Illinois Territory, Maine, New York, North Carolina, Pennsylvania, Tennessee, and Virginia are partially missing.

1820: Name of the household head; free white males and females under 10 years old, between the ages of 10 and 16, 16 and 18, 18 and 26, 26 and 45, and over 45 years old; naturalized aliens; work in the agricultural, commercial, and manufacturing industries; free blacks; slaves; and people (with the exception of American Indians) not taxed. Schedules for Alabama, Arkansas Territory, Missouri, and New Jersey are entirely missing. Those for Georgia, Indiana, Maine, New Hampshire, North Carolina, Ohio, Pennsylvania, and Tennessee are partially missing.

1830: Name of household head; free white people under 5 years old, 10 years old, 15 years old, 20 years old, 30 years old, 40 years old and over; professions; the city, county, town, parish, district, etc., where the census was taken; military veterans who received pensions; deafness, dumbness, and blindness; unnaturalized aliens; free blacks; slaves; and schools.

1840: Name of household head; age; sex; race; slaves; deafness; dumbness; blindness; insanity; idiocy; employment; literacy; and pensioners for Revolutionary or military service.

1850, 1860: At this point, federal censuses began to include more information. For every free person living in the household is a record of name; age; sex; color; occupation; value of real estate owned; birthplace; marital status; school attendance; literacy; convict status; and slaves set free. For each slave there is a record of the slave owner; slave's age, sex, and color, as well as whether the slave was a fugitive or not. The 1860 census includes the number of slave houses and value of personal estate.

1870: This census contains the same information as 1860, as well as month of birth or marriage if occurred within the year; denial of vote for reasons other than rebellion; and whether parents were foreign born.

1880: Indexed alphabetically by name, this census records the name, age, sex, marital status, race, sickness or disability, months unemployed during the year; school attendance, literacy, relationship to the head of the household, and birthplace of person and parents.

1890: The 1890 census was almost completely destroyed by fire and only portions exist.

1900: Address; name; relationship to household head; sex; race; age; marital status; foreign birth; year immigrated to U.S.; naturalization status; school attendance; literacy; birthplace of person and parents; native language; ability to speak English; occupation; home ownership or rental; and original amount of mortgage, balance due, and interest rate.

1910: This offers all the information included in previous censuses, as well as each female's number of children born and number living; language spoken if not English; survivor of Union or Confederate army or navy. It also lists the Indian tribe or band when applicable.

1920: Similar to preceding years, it does not have a separate American Indian listing as the 1910 census did, nor does it indicate how many years married or whether a person served in the Confederate or Union forces during the Civil War.

1930: Address; name; relationship to household head; home ownership or rental; rental fee; radio ownership; farm residence; sex; race; age; marital status; age at first marriage; school attendance; literacy; birthplace of person and parent; native language; year of immigration; naturalization status; ability to speak English; occupation; industry; worker class; veteran status; and for American Indians, whether of full or mixed blood and tribal affiliation.

Most states also have instituted their own censuses. Whenever possible, inspect the census of the state in which your ancestor lived if only to verify the information from the federal census. Census information, as stated previously, is at national archives depositories, and can also be found (e.g., local, county, state) at many historical libraries and public libraries. The National Archives rents census microfilm, as do the Family History Library, Heritage Quest, and other sources.

NON-POPULATION CENSUSES

Accompanying some U.S. population census are mortality schedules taken from 1850 to 1885 that list persons who died the year before the census was taken. If a relative died in 1849, 1859, 1869, and 1879, see the census for the following year for the listing of the person's name, age, sex, occupation, death cause, death date, and county where the person died. Slaves were included in these schedules, but their surnames or the names of slave owners were not. Originals of these schedules are stored at the National Archives or state agencies; the National Society of the Daughters of the American Revolution have those not claimed by the states of Arizona, Colorado, Georgia, Kentucky, Louisiana, Tennessee and the District of Columbia. The Family History Library has copies of most of these. Other censuses to study are agricultural, industrial, and institutional enumerations.

MILITARY RECORDS

The United States has been involved in several military conflicts in its short life, so chances are high that one or more of your male ancestors served in combat. Just think, your ancestor could have played a decisive role in creating the world as we know it! Finding military records will certainly add color and spice to your genealogy.

The number of military records available at the National Archives alone is awe inspiring. A partial summary (not including documents at state and local archives) follows:

1) Coast Guard records

2) Service records for enlisted men in the Marines, Navy, and Army

3) Navy Army Marines officer records

4) Civil War, Mexican War, Spanish-American War, World War I, Philippine Insurrection records

5) Muster rolls for the Army

6) Records of appointees to Annapolis

7) Prisoner of War records

8) Records of soldiers' burials

9) Women solders

National Archives offers the free publication *Military Service Records in the National Archives* that explains its bounty of war records. Of these, genealogists should be on the special look out for three record types: Service records, veterans' benefits, and bounty land grants.

Figure 6: MAJOR AMERICAN MILITARY CONFLICTS

1775–1779	The Revolutionary War
1812–1815	The War of 1812
1846	The Mexican War
1861–1865	The Civil War
1898	The Spanish-American War
1914–1918	World War I
1939–1945	World War II
1950–1953	The Korean Conflict
1964–1972	The War in Vietnam
1990–1991	The Gulf War

SERVICE RECORDS

A World War I draft registration form contained name, age, address, birth date, birth place, citizenship, occupation, employer, dependency supports, next of kin, physical description, father's birth place, marital status, and prior service! (These registration cards can be seen on microfilm in Family History Libraries or the National Archives repository in East Point, Georgia.) Honorable discharge certificates also reveal telling data.

But how do you know whether your relative served in a war? If you don't have any family records, don't give up. Death certificates typically require military service to be recorded. Keep in mind your relative's age and compare that with the dates of all wars and police actions in which America has been involved. The accompanying chart (*See Figure 6*) may be of some help to you.

Basically, all you need to know is which address to write to and which form to use. The more information you can provide about your ancestor the better, but staff members can usually make do with the bare minimum. The amount of information that they can send back to you varies depending upon in which war your ancestor served (some older records are incomplete or lost), but it will surely help in constructing your genealogy.

Your best bet for service records is the National Archives. Be aware that, as with census records, military documents are considered private for 75 years, so you can only request specifically about your ancestor if the record is more than 75 years old. The earliest records, those from the eighteenth and nineteenth century, are often only muster rolls, a form of attendance registers that lists name, rank, and unit.

To obtain a copy of a service record, write to the National Archives, (or e-mail to inquire@nara.gov) and ask for a copy of NATF Form 80. Once you complete and mail back the form, a staff member will search for your ancestor's records and mail you results for a small photocopying fee. To obtain a copy of a service record for a veteran of the Civil War, you can also use NATF Form 80. If your relative served in the Confederacy, you may be out of luck, because the National Archives primarily houses records of the Union soldiers even though it does has some Confederate information, such as Confederate pension records. Instead contact the archives of the states that comprised the Confederacy for their records.

To obtain a copy of a service record that is less than 75 years old, write to the Department of Defense, National

Personnel Records Center, 9700 Page Boulevard, St. Louis, MO 63132-5100 or use Standard Form 180, which is available on the National Archives web site in the section "Order Forms for Military Service and Family History Records" or NARA's Fax-on-Demand system (call 301-731-6905 from a fax machine and follow voice instruction to request document number 2255). Let them know you are related to the veteran for whom you are searching.

Several web sites allow you to search for your ancestor's military records. You can do on-line searches using Everton's On-line SearchBulletin Board System (register by calling 435-752-6095 through your computer and use a major credit card) that uses several databases, even one for U.S. forts! Some web sites that may prove useful are:

American Revolutionary War Soldiers & Their Descendants
http://www.rootsweb.com/~ars/index.htm

Civil War Soldiers and Sailors System
http://www.itd.nps.gov/cwss/

United States Army Military History Institute
http://carlisle-www.army.mil/usamhi/
(This one has soldier photographs from the Civil War and later from which you can order copies.)

VETERAN PENSIONS

Probably the most important military records are pension applications. Of the literally millions of applications, the National Archives has divided them into seven categories: Revolutionary War invalid, Revolutionary War service, Old Wars, War of 1812, Mexican War, Indian Wars, and Civil War and Later.

Many pension applications contain a variety of information, including letters from relatives, friends, and fellow soldiers, birth and marriage certificates . . . anything that would have added credibility to the veteran's pension clam. If the claim was filed by the veteran himself, then it most likely includes vital statistics and a summary of his duties in the Armed Forces. If filed by his widow, then it also includes her vital statistics and the names of their dependents. If it was filed by a dependent, then the application includes the dependent's vital statistics as well.

Female ancestors don't only show up as dependents in military record files. Until the nineteenth century, true, women's main contact with the military was pension application or support employment. Then, in 1890, Civil War nurses became eligible to apply for federal pensions for their own service. Later, women served in World War I, and increased their numbers in World War II through such organizations as the Women Accepted for Volunteer Emergency Services (WAVES), Women Airforce Service Pilots (WASP), and other branches. To find out more, examine records for the individual war department (e.g., army, air force) and indexes.

When trying to find your ancestor's pension application, you must be able to provide the National Archives' staff with the exact state and preferably town or county that your ancestor came from, because of the number of duplicate names on file.

To get a copy of your ancestor's pension application file, or to find out whether one of your ancestors has ever made such a claim, contact the National Archives and request NATF Form 80. If you feel more valuable information was not sent to you, write the National Archives and ask them how much it will cost to obtain a copy of the complete file. They will let you know, and you can then decide whether it is worth the fee.

Don't limit your search to the National Archives only. The Veteran's Administration (1-800-VA7-1000) has many documents of interest, as does The American Legion (http://www.legion.org/libfaq.htm).

BOUNTY LAND GRANTS

Land grants were one way the government rewarded its veterans. Patriots (or their heirs) who fought in wars between the years 1775 and 1855 were entitled to land that was part of the public domain. Besides providing an inducement for men to serve their country, land grants also brought about the migration of people to the western area of the United States.

As to the exact amount, Congress decreed on September 16, 1776, that each colonel was entitled to 500 acres of land; lieutenant colonels, 450 acres; captains, 300 acres; lieutenants, 200 acres; ensigns, 150 acres; and each soldier, 100 acres of land.

Among the information contained in the land grant application files are the veteran's name, rank, unit, service term, age, residence, and sometimes even a physical description of the applicant. If filed by an heir, the file includes the veteran's name, the name of the heir, their relationship, and the place and date of the veteran's death.

Bounty applications are divided into two categories: Revolutionary War and post-Revolutionary War. To obtain a copy of your ancestor's file, write to the National Archives, and, yes, use NATF Form 80.

HOMESTEAD FILES AND OTHER LAND TRANSACTIONS

The federal government also sold or gave away land to ordinary citizens through land grants, patents, and homesteads. Homestead files, housed with the others in the National Archives, contain a claimant's name, age, citizenship, witness testimony, crops grown, and house and tract description.

Deeds, the most common type of land records, are housed locally, and sometimes include information on family relationships, dower rights, and slave ownership. Other land sources are railroad land-sale records to individuals, county land deeds, and county atlas—all found in your state historical library or county offices.

PASSENGER LISTS AND NATURALIZATION RECORDS

With passenger lists, it is possible to find out when your ancestors arrived in the United States as well as what country they left from to get here with passenger lists. Starting in 1820, custom officials at Atlantic

Coast and Mexican gulf ports began preserving daily passenger records. These records eventually ended up in the National Archives and extend into the twentieth century. Fires destroyed lists from the San Francisco port, and lists from before 1820 are just plain scarce.

Passenger lists usually contain the name of the captain and ship; the embarkation port; the port name; ship arrival date; and the name, age, sex, and occupation of each passenger. More recent lists may include a passenger's amount of money, physical description, and health.

Illegible writing, record gaps, and incomplete information and indexing plague passenger lists. Therefore it is best that you know the name of the ship your ancestor came on, the port of entry, and arrival date. With this data, the staff of the National Archives may be able to find your information. You might ask "How can I find these facts?" Fortunately, several books list the names of the millions of passengers who arrived in this country by ship and the dates of their arrival, in particular *Passenger and Immigration Lists Index* (lists over 2.6 million immigrants with entries that include name, age, place and year of arrival, and accompanying family members) updated annually by Gale Research. Other examples of books with passenger lists include:

The Original List of Persons of Quality Who Went from Great Britain to the American Plantations, 1600–1700 (John Hotten)

Dutch Immigrants in U.S. Passenger Manifests: 1820–1880

A List of Emigrants From England to America, 1719–1759 (Jack Kaminkow)

Jewish Immigration to the United States From 1881 to 1910 (Samuel Joseph)

Adler's Directory: A Compilation of Passenger Steamships Sailing From European Ports and Arriving in the Eastern Ports of the United States From 1899–1929.

A new key is the Ellis Island Foundation research center that showcases a computer database using microfilm copies of original handwritten passenger arrival. Most are not available on-line (yet!), but check with the National Archives (www.nara.gov/publications/microfilm/immigrant/immpass.html) to get film numbers for ports. You also can hunt passenger list web sites (e.g., United States, Australia, New Zealand, and Canada) or use general World Wide Web search engines for individual ship names and ports to find the passenger list you need. Another option is to join an Internet discussion group:

Address: theshipslist-d-request@rootsweb.com
Message: subscribe

Address: majordomo@listserv.northwest.com
Message: subscribe emigration ships

Address: immi-grand-d-request@rootsweb.com
Message: subscribe

Naturalization records might be able to help you search for passenger lists, and vice-versa. In other words, if you know the name of the court where your ancestor was naturalized (this can be learned from the list of voters in the county where he lived), you can gain access to naturalization records, which will tell you place and date of birth, date of arrival into the United States, residence, description of the individual, and sometimes the name of the ship on which your ancestor arrived. For years 1781 through 1906 write to the National Archives. For naturalization records after 1906, write to the Immigration and Naturalization Service (119 D Street, N.W., Washington, DC 20536, http://www.ins.usdoj.gov/) and request form N-585. After filling in and returning this form, you will be sent a file with the information you need.

SOCIAL SECURITY RECORDS

The 1935 Social Security Act that provides retirement or survivor death benefits allows today's genealogists to access yesterday's bonanza of application forms, since people born in the mid-1800s onward are documented in Social Security's files. The most common record is an application form for a Social Security Number, Form SS-5, which consists of an applicant's full name, address, age, place of employment, sex, race, signature, and parent's names and birth dates. To receive a copy, fill out form L-997 or post a letter containing all of the information that will help identify the individual, including the person's social security number and a copy of their death certificate. There will be a fee that depends on the amount of information Social Security provides. Write: Social Security Administration, Office of Central Operations—Genealogy, 330 North Greene Street, Baltimore, MD 21235.

When a person is reported deceased, the Social Security Administration enters that name on a computerized index of deceased individuals (Social Security

Death Index), which includes the name, birth and death dates, last zip code, and zip codes of heirs that received death benefits. This comprehensive death index (best for 1960 and on, but does have earlier dates) can help locate death dates and relation connections. It is both on-line at several web sites and at most Family History Centers. For more information on Social Security resources, see *The Social Security Administration* site (http://www.ssa.gov) or *The Social Security & Genealogy FAQ* (http:// www.rechtman. com/ssafaq.htm).

PASSPORTS

Although passports were first issued in 1795, they were not required for travel to foreign countries until the mid-1800s. These documents include the individual's full name, birth date, residence, and departure dates. Many include physical descriptions; recent ones include photographs. Passport applications are available through the Family History Library. The State Department, which is responsible for U.S. passports, stores all processed passports in the National Archives and will furnish copies for a fee.

FEDERAL BUREAU OF INVESTIGATION RECORDS

The Federal Bureau of Investigation (FBI) has kept records on people since 1908 for a variety of reasons. If you think one of your relatives might be in its file cabinet, write:

> Federal Bureau of Investigation
> Attn: Freedom of Information — Privacy Act Unit
> Office of Public and Congressional Affairs
> 935 Pennsylvania Avenue N. W.
> Washington, DC 20535-0001 USA

Make sure you include proof that your relative is dead or that the person's age exceeds 100 years, all known facts about the individual, a request to search records, and a statement that you will pay for the information (e.g., I will pay up to $__ for reasonable fees)— the FBI expects you to cough up at least $25 for research expenses and photocopies. You do not need to show proof that you are related to the individual. To find out more see the FBI web site (http://www.fbi.gov).

HIRING A PROFESSIONAL GENEALOGIST— THE RIGHT DECISION FOR YOU?

By now, some of you may feel overwhelmed by the complexity of putting together a comprehensive family history. As a result, you might come to a point where you decide you would like to hire a professional genealogist to, for instance, translate a foreign language in records, obtain inaccessible records (e.g., membership, geographical), meet time deadlines, or simply because you have reached a dead end and have nowhere else to turn.

If you absolutely require the services of a professional genealogist expect the following:

1) An initial consultation with the professional, to provide any information you have already acquired and to discuss exactly what additional information you want provided.

2) A discussion on the professional's special skills, such as foreign language mastery or archive familiarity.

3) Ancestral and family group charts filled out with information citation and photocopies of original sources, if possible, along with a detailed invoice of search expenses.

4) Outlining of the fees, time length to complete task, and start date.

Often, the best way to find a researcher is through local libraries. Another way is to consult a genealogist listed through accrediting organizations, such as:

Board for Certification of Genealogists
P. O. Box 5816
Falmouth, VA 22403-5816
http://www.genealogy.org/~bcg/

Association of Professional Genealogists
P. O Box 40393
Denver, CO 80204-0393
http://www.apgen.org.

Family History Library
Accredited Genealogist
35 North West Temple Street
Salt Lake City, UT 84150

You will also probably find certain professionals advertised in the genealogical periodicals, and they should be legitimate because the periodicals usually research the credentials of those who advertise. Be wary, though, of "professionals" who advertise in non-genealogical periodicals, as a high percentage are frauds. They usually compile a single genealogy for everyone with the same last name and don't check to see if this is your true line of descent.

Chapter Ten

SEARCHING FOR ANCESTORS IN FOREIGN COUNTRIES

*T*ypically, the vital event records you need overseas are in the actual town where your relatives lived. Many are still at the church where your ancestors worshipped; others are in civil record offices, and the staff there may be helpful or not because your genealogy search probably is not part of their job duties.

Often, these records (or their duplicates) have been sent on to a regional or national repository. The web site *Repositories of Primary Source* (http://www.uidaho.edu/special-collections/Other.Repositories.html) lists web sites and contact information for libraries and archives in the United States, Canada, Latin America, Caribbean, Europe, Asia and the Pacific, African, and the Near East. For instance, the European section includes the following countries: Andorra, Austria, Belgium, Czech Republic, Denmark, Estonia, Faro, Finland, France, Germany, Greece, Hungary, Iceland, Ireland, Italy, Latvia, Lithuania, Luxembourg, Macedonia, Netherlands, Norway, Poland, Russia, Slovenia, Spain, Sweden, Switzerland, United Kingdom, and Yugoslavia. *World-Wide Genealogy Resources* (http://www.genhomepage.com/world.html) is also a good starting point for searches.

The Family History Library and its branches in the United States have an amazing amount of these primary records stored in foreign archives. There are copies of these records and other site-specific information at Family History Library branches world-wide that also may be of help to you.

Overcoming the language barrier is, of course, a roadblock in overseas searches. Fortunately, people in other countries often speak English. You can also employ translators, or even use the World Wide Web to convert other languages into English. The AltaVista search engine (http://www.altavista.com) for instance, provides on-line translation on its homepage. Just type in text, pick a language, then click the Translate button. Ideally, this will work for your purposes. In reality, you may have to consult with a person familiar with the language. Contact a local university for language translators, or use the Internet or a genealogical society to find the language specialist you need.

It also is a good idea to contact a country-specific genealogical society in the United States before you begin your overseas search. This is especially true when dealing with countries experiencing political strife and changing boundaries.

LIST OF SOURCES, COUNTRY BY COUNTRY

The following list is by no means complete. But, it will give you an idea of ancestor hunting abroad!

AMERICAN SAMOA

Vital events have been on record since 1900. For a copy, contact:

Registrar of Vital Statistics
Vital Statistics Section
Government of American Samoa
Pago Pago, AS 96799
684-633-1222, ext. 214

AUSTRALIA

The government mandated civil registration of births, marriages, and deaths in 1856. These records can be obtained from the capital city of the state in which the event happened. Before civil registration, this information was recorded in parish registers, which are now at state libraries and the Family History Centres in Australia. Australia has poor census records, since so many have been destroyed. Other sources to search include Public Record Offices for passenger records at the time when your ancestor arrived, and wills. Addresses for local, state, territory, and national repositories can be found at the Australian Family History Compendium (http://www.cohsoft.com.au/afhc/#addresses). Also contact:

> National Archives of Australia
> Queen Victoria Terrace
> Canberra, ACT 2610
> Australia
> http://www.naa.gov.au/index.htm

AUSTRIA

Similar to most European countries, the recording of vital events in Austria began in local parishes. Ministers began documenting such events in the mid-sixteenth century, and all churches did so starting in 1784. To find vital records from 1938 to the present and civil documents, contact the registrars of the town in which your ancestor lived. Records from 1835–1959 may be found in the Central Archives. Austria also has an archive for military information in Vienna, which you can contact at:

> Kriegsarchiv
> Nottendorfergasse 2-4
> A-1030 Wien

Interestingly, Austria has kept records on employ-ment, which is on microfilm at several Family History Centers in Austria. You may also want to research Hamburg passenger lists as many Austrians emigrated from this port. The web site *German Genealogy: Austria* http://www.genealogy.net/gene/reg/AUT/aus-tria-en.html) offers further information on the fine points of Austrian genealogy, as well as addresses.

BELGIUM

Starting in the early 1600s, the Catholic clergy kept vital records for Belgium citizens until civil reg-istration in 1795. These records, now available in town halls and many state archives, are in Dutch, French, Latin, or German languages. The Belgium national archives are:

Archives generales du Royaume
Rue de Ruysbroeck 1000
Bruxelles
Belgium

An excellent web site for Belgium genealogy is *How to Find Your Roots in Belgium* (http://www.ping.be/picavet/). Also contact:

Genealogical Society of Flemish Americans
18740 Thirteen Mile Road
Roseville, MI 48066

CANADA

Although civil records in Canada do exist back to the 1860s (even to the 1620s in some Quebec locations), the government did not enforce civil registration country-wide until the 1920s. Canada does not keep its civil registration records in one central office. Instead, vital statistics are filed with provincial and territorial offices (see Appendix for locations and record contents). They may also be found in archives, as are church records, census results (1871 and onward), and passenger lists dating back to 1865. Also contact the Canadian National Archives, which does have some information on-line (e.g., Index to the 1871 Census of Ontario, Dominion Land Grants).

National Archives of Canada
395 Wellington Street
Ottawa, ON K1AON3
Canada
http://www.archives.ca/

Another source is the United Church Archives. In 1925, the Methodist, Presbyterian, and Congregational churches joined to form the United Church of Canada. Contact the United Church Archives, which has the past records of these three churches

United Church of Canada
Victoria University
Queen's Park Crescent East
Toronto, Ontario M5S 1K7

and also see *Sources for Genealogical Research in Canada* (http://www.king.igs.net/~bdmlhm/cangenealogy.html) and:

American-Canadian Genealogical Society
P. O. Box 668
Manchester, NH 03105

THE PEOPLES' REPUBLIC OF CHINA

Because of ancestor worship in China (as well as other countries), it is often possible to find an already completed genealogy of your ancestors. That is, if it wasn't burnt during the 1950s when the Chinese government burned many "dangerous" records, or if the government will release documents.

The heart of Chinese record searching is at each city's population bureau. These offices hold marriage, birth, and death certificates. You may reach one of these by writing: Population Registration, Ministry of Public Security, (Name of city where you are searching), China. Another place to write is the National Central Library (care of the Chief Librarian) in Taipei, Taiwan to see whether there is a published genealogy on your family. If this search proves unfruitful, try to contact any living relatives in China for their private genealogical records, visit cemeteries, look at a *fang-chih* (local history), and read the walls at ancestral worshiping halls that are adorned with ancestor's names.

CUBA

Cubans first immigrated to work in U.S. industries. During the political unrest of the 1950s, many Cubans immigrated, especially after Fidel Castro took power. The greatest exodus was in 1980 when more than 100,000 Cubans left during the Mariel boat lift. Since then thousands leave each year. For information on tracing ancestors, contact:

Cuban Genealogical Society
P. O. Box 2650
Salt Lake City, UT 82110

CZECH REPUBLIC

With the fall of Communism, the country known as Czechoslovakia divided into two countries, Czech Republic and Slovakia. Catholic and Protestant clergy began recording vital events in the seventeenth century, and your ancestor's records are still available in his or her local parish. Civil authorities began recording vital events in 1950, and these records are stored in the central archives of the two countries. For a small fee, you can ask these two agencies to search for records:

Ministry of the Interior
Archivni Sprava
Tridadr
Milady Horakove, 133
166 21 Prague

Ministry of the Interior
Department of Archives
Krizkova 7
811 04 Bratislava, Slovakia

or you may want to first contact:

Czechoslovak Genealogical Society International
Library
Minnesota Genealogical Society Library
5768 Olson Memorial Hwy.
Golden Valley, MN 55422
612-595-7799

DENMARK

In 1645, the Lutheran church began keeping vital event records, which are now at local parishes and at the Family History Library, as are Roman Catholic (1685 on), Reformed (1747 on), and Jewish (1814 on) records. In the nineteenth century, the government took over. You can find these records, court proceedings, censuses (1787 on), and draft lists (1789 on) at Denmark's National Archives (see their on-line publication "Roots in Denmark"):

Rigsarkivet
Rigsdagsgarden 9
DK-1218 Kobenhavn
Denmark
mailbox@ra.sa.dk
http://www.sa.dk/ra/uk/uk.htm

As late as 1850, many rural families had no permanent last name, because they used the patronymic naming system. Therefore, when searching Danish records it is a good practice to have your ancestor's birthplace, emigration year, Danish version of name, and a Danish certificate (e.g., marriage license). Postmarked letters also can help pinpoint a relative's residence so you can use parish records.

Balkan and Eastern European American Gen.
Society
4838 Mission Street
San Francisco, CA 94112

Estonian American National Council
Estonian House
243 E. 34th Street
New York, NY 10016

ENGLAND

Although vital record keeping began in England in the 1500s, civil registration did not start until 1837. Contact the Family Records Centre, 1 Mydlleton Street, Islington, London, ECIR IUW, United Kingdom for these records and for census data from 1841–1891 (also available at the Family History Libraries). For vital records before 1837, you will have to search church archives at local parishes or contact the Society of Genealogists, 37 Harrington Gardens, Kensington, London, SW74JX, England. If your family did not belong to the Church of England, the Society can give you leads to other religious storage sites.

Probate records can be obtained from:

Probate Department
Principal Registry
First Avenue House
42-49 High Holbasin
London WX IV 6NP
United Kingdom

FINLAND

In the 1600s, parish ministers began recording vital events. Civil records only came into effect at the end of World War I, and Finnish citizens are not required to use them. If they wish, they may still record events solely through the church. For church records written after 1850, seek out the individual parish where your ancestor worshiped. For records before 1850, or for civil records, contact:

National Repository Library
P. O. Box 1710
SE-70421 Kuopio
http://varasto.uku.fi/english/

FRANCE

Not only does France have some of the oldest records in Europe, but it also commenced systematic civil registration of vital events following the French Revolution. The National Archives of France stores these records and its staff may be able to answer your questions. The earliest religious registers appeared around 1334. These and peerage lists, land records, and assorted other records were written in Latin. Until the end of the eighteenth century, local clergy maintained vital records (since 1539, for Catholics; 1559, Protestants). Now, these documents are housed in local town halls ("mairies") and regional archives (contact the National Archives for addresses), as are censuses dating to 1836. Records less than 100 years are usually not available to the public. The National Archives also has army records and immigration documents. It also has probate records that go back more than 600 years, although newer records may be at local archives.

> Centre d'accueil et de recherche des Archives nationales
> 11
> rue des Quatre-Fils
> 75003 Paris
> France
> http://www.culture.fr/culture/sedocum/caran.htm

You may also want to contact:

American-French Genealogical Society
P. O. Box 2113
Pawtucket, RI 02861-0113
http://www.afgs.org/

GERMANY

Professional genealogists consider Germany to be one of the most difficult countries in which to trace family roots. The difficulty arises from the shifting boundaries within and around the present country of Germany that resulted from wars and religious conflicts. Before embarking on serious study, it is essential to know the religion of your ancestor. With that information, you can contact the appropriate church.

The Lutherans began recording vital events in 1540; the Roman Catholics, 1563, and Reformed, 1650. In 1876, civil registration replaced church records and the records stored in a town archive and registrar's office ("Standesamt"). Each province also has an archive where records are stored. Other clues can be found in emigration records. Between 1850 and 1930, Hamburg was the main emigration port, with records listing a passenger's name, residence, destination, traveling companions, and ship name.

German Genealogical Society of America
21256 Wright Avenue, #C-9
La Verne, CA 91750

Immigrant Genealogical Society Library
German Research
1310-B W. Magnolia Boulevard
Burbank, CA 91510-7369
818-848-3122
http://feefhs.org/igs/frg-igs.html

American Historical Society of Germans from Russia Archives
631 D Street
Lincoln, NE 68502
402-474-3363
http://www.ahsgr.org

GREECE

Know what town your relative was born, and your search is half-way done! Church records date to the early 1800s and are still kept in local parishes, while civil records (since 1925) are in the town's local archives.

GUAM

The Office of Vital Statistics has vital event records dating to October 16, 1901. Contact:

Office of Vital Statistics
Department of Public Health
Government of Guam
P. O. Box 2816
Agana, GU, M. I. 96910
671-734-4589

HUNGARY

Clergy from both the Roman Catholic and Reformed churches documented vital events from 1695 to 1895. These records are stored in the local parishes (and have been microfilmed by the Family History Library), while civil records (1895 to present) are in town registrars. Many Hungarians also emigrated from the Hamburg port, so check those passenger lists, too. (See the web site *Genealogy Research in Hungary* (http://www.bogardi.com/) for available research sources, such as the 1891 national census, place loca-tors, surname changes, Old Budapest city directories, etc.) Before you begin your search, remember that the aftermath of World War I caused about half of the Austrian-Hungarian population to be citizens of Austria, Hungary, Czechoslovakia, Yugoslavia, Romania, the Soviet Union, Poland, and Italy.

ICELAND

Vital events have been recorded by local parish ministers since 1746, and these documents can be found in Iceland's National Archives. There, too, censuses that have been taken every ten years since 1703 list emigrants to the United States and Canada, as well as other records that date to the 9th century. For more information, contact:

National Archives
Reykjavik, Iceland

Icelandic Genealogical Society
http://www.vortex.is/aett/English.html

INDIA

India has no official birth, marriage, or death certificates. The British began recording vital event information in 1698 for both Catholic and Protestant countrymen. This information is now stored in the Oriental and India Office Collections (96 Euston Rd., London NW1 2DB United Kingdom, http://www. bl.uk/collections/oriental/colls.html) at the British Library. The Family History Library also has microfilmed many of these records.

IRELAND

Church records for either Protestants or Catholics are most easily found in local parishes. Basically, Roman Catholic church records start around 1830, Protestant marriage records in 1845, and civil registration since 1864. For many years, Roman Catholics had to be covert in their religious practices. This fact, plus the 1922 fire that burned vast numbers of records, and the destruction of the 1901 and 1911 census, make searching Irish ancestors difficult. On the positive side, the *Irish History Foundation* (http://irishroots.net/) has set up heritage centers in each county, which are listed on its web site, to aid genealogists. Since 1990, the Foundation has been computerizing records and now has a wealth of information, including gravestone inscriptions, work house records, and other specialized details. Numerous records and publications can also be found at:

> National Archives
> Bishop Street
> Dublin 8
> Republic of Ireland
> http://www.nationalarchives.ie

Also contact:

> Irish American Genealogical. Society
> P. O. Box 26507
> Prescott Valley, AZ 86312

ITALY

Between 1880 and 1920 more than 4 million Italians came to the United States, which makes Italians one of the United States' largest immigrant groups. In general, records are stored locally rather than centrally in Italy. Civil registration of vital events began in the 1800s and was country-wide around 1860. Happily, these records can contain several generations of names, occupations, and other detailed information. See the web site *Civil Record Repositiories in Italy* (http://www.italgen.com/civrec/civilrec.htm) for exact locations. Before that period (and even during because many churches still kept their own records), look for parochial records (baptism, marriage, death, and the church census known as "stato delle anime"). Records, for the most part, are in the localities where your ancestors lived or at a regional Archive of State, usually in the provincial capital. Expect to find church offering records, land donations, wills, feudal taxes, tenant rents, military service, and agricultural reports.

Italian Genealogical Group
7 Grayon Drive
Dix Hills
New York, New York 11746
http://www.italiangen.org

Italian Genealogical Society of America
P. O. Box 8571
Cranston, R. I. 02920-8571

JAMAICA AND THE WEST INDIES

Civil registration began in 1880. Those records and earlier Anglican church records are catalogued by parish and stored in the Island Record Office, Spanish Town, Jamaica. The Family History Libraries have microfilmed those records, so you should be able to access them without visiting or writing to Jamaica. See *Family History Jamaica* (http://users.pullman.com/mitchelm/jamaica.htm) for more information. Much of this information is also in *Jamaican Ancestry: How to Find Out More* (Heritage Books, 1998) by Madeleine Mitchell, the author of the fore-mentioned web site.

Thirty countries comprise the West Indies. The news group soc.genealogy.west-indies, which is linked to the Caribbean-L group (e-mail: CARIBBEAN-L-request@rootsweb.com and send the message "subscribe"), offers a wealth of information as well as surname lists. See also Puerto Rico and Virgin Island in this chapter's listing.

JAPAN

The keystone of Japanese genealogy is the *koseki*, the family registry. It records births, deaths, parents, marriages, marital status, emigration, and other information on Japanese citizens. The *koseki shouhon* is the short version of the family tree and is part of the *koseki touhon*, the registry of an entire family extending through time. The usual *koseki shouhon* lists one person's name, that person's parents, birth date and order in the family, places where the person has lived, and the person who submitted the information. The government requires Japanese citizens to notify local authorities when moving, so the *koseki* should have a well-documented family migration trail.

Koseki information is stored in the family's "hometown," even if they no longer live there, although some families do transfer records. Many *koseki*, similar to other official Japanese documents, date to the reign of an Emperor.

Theoretically, you would contact a local ward office in the place where your relatives lived, give the name of the family member and your relationship to the family, and then obtain the *Koseki* you want. However, *koseki* contents are considered extremely private and officials will only release the information if presented with a reason they find acceptable; genealogy isn't always a good enough reason. Decisions vary from city to city.

Therefore, first contact any family members in the United States or Japan to see whether they have a copy of the family *koseki*. Going in person to request a *koseki* and asking in advance what information you may need to provide is your second best chance. Obviously, that is expensive and impractical. If you do write officials, try to have the letter written in Japanese. Every town or city is in a prefecture, which is the same as a state in the United States. Look on the Internet for the municipal addresses of the town or city first; if not listed, look through the prefecture's listing.

LATIN AMERICA

When researching roots in Latin America, see holdings in the *Hispanic Reading Room* (http://rr.hispanic/

hisp2.htm#hisp.kweb.lco.gov) of the Library of Congress first. The web site *Hispanic Genealogical Research* (http://www.genealogia.com) has several search leads, including libraries in Brazil, Chile, Columbia, Peru, Uruguay, and Venezuela. Many of these countries have Internet mail discussion groups and compile information on individual surnames. And, while Spanish is the predominant language, other languages are spoken, and Central and Latin American Internet resources commonly offer information in different languages. Brazil is the only Portuguese-speaking country, but, it too has Internet information in English. (See the web site Genealogia, http://genealogia.com.br/english/Eng_sites.html, for Brazilian genealogy information on-line, e.g., churches, maps, archives, libraries, and surname lists.)

LUXEMBOURG

Local parishes hold the key to your search in Luxembourg. Each parish lists its "Presbytere" (priest) in the Luxembourg Telephone Directory, and you may contact the priest for information. One web site loaded with good search tips is *Luxembourg Genealogy* (http://www.luxembourg.co.uk/genealog. html). Also contact the Luxembourg Society of Genealogy and Heraldry, which has more than 3,000 print sources relating to genealogy in Luxembourg, an index of marriages before 1802, a run-down of parish records and censuses of Luxembourg, members' genealogy charts, and "family reconstructions" for numerous towns.

The Luxembourg Society of Genealogy and
Heraldry
Castle of Mersch/Third Floor
P. O. Box 118-L-7502 Mersch
Luxembourg

MEXICO

Censuses were done on a regular basis starting in
1895. The Family History Library has the entire 1921
Mexican census available and another from 1819–1839.
Because the U.S. Mexican border was open until the
first part of the twentieth century, no records regarding
immigration are available for that time period, although
Immigration and Naturalization has lists of border-
crossing privileges from 1903–1953. Search out notary
records, an important research source, because they
gave "legal stamp of approval" to all transactions—
taxes, applications, apprenticeships, rentals, dowry letters, payments, certificates, etc. These notarial records
are stored in various archives. The main archive is:

Archivo Genreal de Notorias de Distrito
Mexico City, Mexico

A good starting part for genealogy tips are:
Hispanic Ancestral Research
P. O. Box 5294
Fullerton, CA 92635

Hispanic Genealogical Society
P. O. Box 231271
Houston, TX 77223

THE NETHERLANDS

Searching for ancestors in the Netherlands means searching for archives! To find what you need, you may have to contact the local registrars' office (birth, marriages, and deaths from 1900 on) or city (civil records from 1812–1902); church records (from 1758–1811); provincial records (most are from 1758–1902); or the national archives. For specific contact informaiton for these many archives (plus private and specialist archives!), see *The Dutch Archives* (http://ourworld.compuserve.com/homepages/paul-van/dutcharc.htm). Another repository is the Central Bureau Voor Genealogie that has an extensive library on genealogy and heraldry, more than 60,000 genealogies, millions of newspaper cuttings about vital events from 1795 to the present, and microfilms of thousands of church and municipal registers.

Central Bureau Voor Genelaogie
Box 11755
NL-2502
The Hague
The Netherlands
http://www.cbg.nl/english.htm

Of special interest is the Bevolking (population) register that can help trace the genealogy of every citizen of the Netherlands back to the year 1811. Also look for national emigration lists that were compiled beginning in 1847 and list a passenger's name, marital status, residence, destination, and age. Also contact:

Dutch Family Heritage Society
2463 Ledgewood Drive
West Jordan, UT 84084-5738
801-967-8400

NORWAY

Tracing ancestors in Norway is much like finding your roots in Sweden. Be aware of the importance of church records from local parishes, and of patronymic naming systems used until the end of the nineteenth century. Norway did not begin recording vital events until the mid-1940s, so you will have to rely on church files that have documents dating to the late 1600s. Regional archives also hold these records besides immigration records, probate records, and property deeds. For current contact information, see the Repositories of Primary Sources listed at the beginning of this chapter. You may also want to contact:

Norwegian-American Genealogical Society
5768 Olson Memorial Hwy.
Golden Valley, MN 55422

PANAMA CANAL

To obtain birth, death, marriage, and divorce records from 1904–1979, send inquiries to:

Canal Zone
Panama Canal Commission
Vital Statistics Clerk
APOAA 34011

For births after 1979 within the former Canal Zone, send requests to:

USA MEDDAC Panama
HSXU-PA
Unit 7139
APOAA 34004

POLAND

Poland has been far larger and far smaller than it is now. Through the last several centuries, Poland, Russia, Germany, Lithuania, and neighboring countries have shifted boundaries. Church records were written in Latin, Polish, Russian, German, Russian, Latin, or Ukrainian depending on the area and religion. Roman Catholic records before the twentieth century are stored in dioces and archives (several have not been transferred from the original parish) and may contain some Protestant records. Many Catholic, Lutheran, and some Jewish church records are stored at the State Archives. Escaping Germans in 1945 took some Lutheran church records to Germany where they are stored at:

Evangelisches Zentralarchiv
Jebenstraße 3
D-10623
Berlin
Germany

Civil registration records older than 100 years are in the State Archives. Later ones are at "town halls" that comprise several former civil registration offices, so records may be from an area rather than one town. Records from areas that once belonged to Poland can be found in the archives at Ukraine, Belarus, and Lithuania. Some records from former German provinces are now stored in Germany at:

Standesamt I
Rückerstraße 0
D-10119
Berlin, Germany

A great number of records in Polish and German archives are now available in Family History Centers. For further information, contact genealogical societies and records in the United States:

Polish Genealogical Society of America
Polish Museum
984 Milwaukee Ave
Chicago, IL 60622-4199

Polish Archives
St. Mary's College
Orchard Lake, MI 48033

PORTUGAL

Genealogical records for Portugal are similar to those of Spain. Local parishes maintained vital records form the mid-sixteenth century onward, but these records have not been transferred to major archives, so you would have to contact the town in which your ancestor lived. Civil authorities began registering vital events in 1878, and these records are in the offices of local officials. To get started, contact:

American-Portuguese Genealogical Society
P. O. Box 644
Taunton, MA 02780

PUERTO RICO

Before 1885, the Catholic parish churches kept vital records. After that date, the government kept records on vital statistics. For events earlier than 1931, contact the *Demographic Registrar* in the municipality where your relative lived. See the web site *Demographic Registrars* (http://www.topuertorico.org/reference/demogra.html) or *Pueblos de Puerto Rico* (http://pueblos-de-puertorico. com) for a listing of the 72 municipalities. For those after 1931, send requests to:

Departamento de Salud
Registro Demografico
P. O. Box 11854
San Juan, PR 00910

Superior District Courts keep the records of wills, deeds, and legal documents of one or more municipalities.

RUSSIA AND THE FORMER SOVIET UNION

Finding your roots in the republics that once formed the U.S.S.R. is no easy task. Many countries there today still engage in sporadic warfare, and because of ever-changing boundaries, it is sometimes difficult to know exactly in which country to begin your search. The public has only recently had access to the records of republics that make up the former Soviet Union and its now-independent satellite countries: Albania, Bulgaria, Czechoslovakia, Hungary, Poland, Romania, and Yugoslavia.

Abundant records exist about the citizens of these countries, but the problem is finding them. You could contact archives; however, most do not have the staff to research for you, and records typically are not indexed. Many archives also do not have copying machines, nor staff who speak English. To find a listing of all of Russia's archives, see the *Archivum* (Volume 98) at larger genealogical libraries.

The Family History Library continues to microfilm records in these countries, so the future should bring more record availability. Presently, the Library has filmed records in Armenia, Belarus, Estonia, Georgia, Lithuania, Moldovia, Russia, and Ukraine. These records are in Russian, Polish, German, and Latin. The older ones are handwritten in the old Russian alphabet, which is difficult to read.

If the Library doesn't have the records you need or you need help in translation, consider asking an expert for help. Formed in 1992, Russian-American Genealogical Archival Services (RAGAS) (1929 eighteenth Street NW, 1112, Washington, DC, 20009, http://feefhs.org/ragas/frgragas.thml) is an organization that helps people obtain archive information in Russia, Ukraine, Belarus, and Estonia. The Russian-Baltic Information Center (BLITZ, see web site at http://feeghs.org/blitz/blitzgrr.html) also researches historic archives, particularly St.

Petersburg and Moscow, and they can provide translation services. This commercial research service requires an initial fee for searches. Also try Cyndislist (http://www.cyndislist.com), Russian-related genealogical societies, or the Avotaynu journal for individual researchers who may be able to help you.

In regard to Russia, early in the eighteenth century local parishes began keeping vital records (Russian Orthodox, 1722; Roman Catholic, 1826; Muslim, 1828; Evangelical Lutheran, 1832; Jewish, 1835; Baptist, 1879) known as Metrical Books (metriki). Besides the local copy, another copy was usually sent to a central civil office. But when revolutionaries overthrew the czar, various religious organizations were stripped of their power. At this time, civil registration of vital events began and those records are now stored at local registrars' offices and in centralized archives. These large volumes were organized by year and within that year, by parishes that could have a German or Russian name.

Equally chock full of genealogical information are the revision lists (revizskiye skazaki) that identify family groups and their residences. In 1719, Peter the Great started these lists to obtain taxes and used military forces to fine and torture local officials who did not submit lists. The military was called off for 1761 revision listings, the first to include females.

Family lists (posemeinye spiski) and local census records pick up in 1860 and extend to 1917. The only universal census was done in 1897 when, in the midst of winter, 150,000 census takers polled Russians for their name, age, sex, religion, social class, occupation, literacy, military status, relationship, disabilities, and native tongue. This information is stored in district archives.

Also of interest are "serf lists" that were conducted starting in 1650 until 1861. These and other records can be found in:

Central State Archives
Vydorgskaya 3
125212
Russia

SCOTLAND

The Church of Scotland is the Presbyterian Church. Local parishes have maintained records since 1690 (in some places, even earlier to 1650). Track down the records at your ancestor's local parish, which may not have baptismal records, because baptism cost parishioners a fee they may not have wanted to pay. Also, other denominations may not be as extensively recorded in local parishes. Or try General Registers's Office, which offers a searchable index of births and marriages (1553–1897), deaths (1855–1897), and the 1881 and 1891 census, for probate records and census records (starting in 1841). You might want to inquire first at the Family History Library, as their collection of Scottish records is extensive.

General Register Office
New Register House
Edinburgh, EH1 3YT
Scotland
research@nas.gov.uk
http://www.open.gov.uk/gros.groshome.htm

Spain

From 1570 until 1870 the Spanish Catholic church maintained all vital records on a parish-by-parish basis— all 19,000 parishes! *The Guidebook of the Spanish Church* (volume 14) indexes these records and can be found at larger genealogical libraries. When civil registration replaced the church as the keeper of vital events records, the records were then stored with the registrar of each town. Spain has a wealth of archives and libraries, each specializing in certain areas. The Archives of the Indies (Seville) has 14 million records of military expeditions to the American continent and passenger lists to the Americas, and Archives of the Crown of Aragon (Barcelona) has the oldest church records. The National Archives has the most genealogical records, including documents from the Inquisition, which could prove helpful in tracing your roots if you are not of Catholic descent. Write to:

Archivo General de Indias
Avenida de la Constitucion
41003 Sevilla Andalucia
Spain

Archivo de la Corona de Aragon
Carrer Comtes 2
08002 Barcelona, Cataluna
Spain

Archivo Historico Nacional
Calle Serrano, 115
28006 Madrid
Spain

SWEDEN

Swedish emigration to the United States began in 1638. The mid-1840s marked the beginning of a tidal wave of Swedish emigration, when population and agricultural hardships at home sent them looking for new homes. So massive was this emigration that the Swedish government started the Emigrant Institute in Vaxjo, Sweden to amass all materials to its departed citizens. The Institute has also microfilmed American records. In Smaland, the House of Emigrants also has archives relating to Swedish emigration history.

The House of Emigrants
P. O. Box 201
S351 04
Vaxjo, Sweden

As for Swedish records, the good news is that church records have been kept since 1608. The bad news is that before the 1870s, these records were kept in a Gothic script. Also, because of Swedish naming practices there are few surnames, and patronymics was used until the nineteenth century, which makes following a wrong lead easy to do. Along with vital event records, parish ministers kept household rolls (*husforhorslangder*), similar to census reports, that are now stored in city and regional archives. Probate records, too, date back hundreds of years, and in 1867 the Swedish government kept immigration records for citizens moving to America. To start tracing Swedish relatives, contact:

Riksarkivet (National Archives)
P. O. Box 12541
Fryrvekarbacken 13-17
S-102 29 Stockholm
Sweden
http://www.ra.se

Swedish American Genealogist
P. O. Box 2186
Winter Park, FL 32790
407-647-4292

Swedish Pioneer Historical Society
5125 North Spaulding Avenue
Chicago, IL 60625

SWITZERLAND

Protestant churches began keeping vital event records in 1525, and Roman Catholics in 1580. Civil registration began in 1876. The government also kept "family registers," which contained records on extended families. The Swiss have a pride in heritage that has resulted in an impressive record-keeping system. Knowing the town of your relative's birth will make your search easier, even if the relative moved away. Contact the town registrar for records dating to 1876. If you want records older than that, contact the National Archives, which will direct you to the right church archives.

National Archives
Arvhivstrasse 4
3003 Bern
Switzerland

If you don't know the town in which your ancestor was born or lived, look through *The Family Name Book of Switzerland*, which will show you how to trace the town through your ancestor's surname. This book is readily available at larger genealogical libraries. Also contact:

Swiss Genealogical Society
Case Postale 54
CH 3608 Thun
Switzerland

VIRGIN ISLANDS

Overseen in part by the United States, the Virgin Islands has a long history. Birth and death records are on file at the Registrar of Vital Statistics, Memorial Hospital, Christiansted, St. Croix, VIT 00820 since 1840. Marriage records are at the Territorial Court of the Virgin Islands, P. O. Box 929, Christiansted, St. Croix, VI 00820. For information on other records, contact 340-774-9000, ext 4621 or 4623.

WALES

Wales has been part of England since 1536. Therefore, look to English records when tracing Welsh ancestors. Once you have an ancestor's name, the place the individual lived, and one date (hopefully), start in London at the Public Record Office (Family Records Centre 1 Myddelton Street, London EC1R 1UW). Next, try the National Library of Wales (Aberystwyth, Fyfed SY23 3BU). Many records throughout Wales have been consolidated here, including marriage licenses, probate records, tithe maps, estate records, and pedigree books. Of special interest are the parish registers from more than 400 parishes that contain names, ages, relationships, etc., dating to 1538. Parish registers can also be found in Country Records Offices. Roman Catholic registers, most dating only from the mid-nineteenth century, are still held in local churches.

Vital event registration began in 1837. But until 1875, there was no penalty for not registering, so omissions may exist for early registers. These events are arranged alphabetically in quarterly indexes. Obtain copy certificates from the General Registor Office (see address of Family Records Centre) or the Superintendent Registrar for the district in which the event occurred.

As in England, the government has taken a census every 10 years from 1801 (except 1941), and this information is available to the public after 100 years. Names were not listed until 1841, but in 1851 more information was detailed, including place of birth, which can lead researchers to the appropriate parish for earlier records. County libraries have microfilm copies of their own censuses; contact the Census Room of the Public Record Office, Land Registry Building, Portugal Street, London WC2 for all censuses. Note that Welsh county boundaries were redrawn in 1974, a move that reduced thirteen counties into eight.

While researching, keep an open mind about surname spellings. A Welsh surname may have a variety of spellings. A current "Griffith" may also be known as "Gruffydd" or "Gruffudd." When checking alphabetical listings, be aware that the entry may be under the first name depending on local custom, or may be identified as the "son of" a father by "ab," "ap," or the possessive "s," exemplified in the popular Welsh surname Jones (son of John).

YUGOSLAVIA

In the former country of Yugoslavia, the government took over vital event recording from the churches in 1946. Each region has its own archive, but because of continual warring, genealogical searches are probably improbable. Look for genealogical groups in the United States, such as:

Croation Migration
1062 E. 62nd Street
Cleveland, OH 44103

Chapter Eleven

SPECIAL GENEALOGICAL CHALLENGES

*T*he availability of written records facilitates ancestor tracing. However, in some situations, records were not kept or have been lost or destroyed. That doesn't make the search impossible. It just adds a challenge to the search! In the United States, adoptees, African Americans, Jews, Native-Americans, and women all encounter record challenges for which we have some search tips.

ADOPTEES

People who are adopted face a challenge in finding their roots that is, quite frankly, difficult to overcome.

But because of the growing upsurge of adoptees who want to find their biological parents, the task is much easier than it once was.

The first thing you should know (or perhaps already know) is that adoption records in most states are still considered private, and only an order of the court can give an adult adoptee the right to view them. Before 1917, adoption records were, for the most part, open until states began sealing them at the demand of social reformers, especially the Child Welfare League. Record availability differs, but, in general, most adoption records before 1930 are open to the public. For those dealing with sealed records, there are quite a few books on the market that can give you ideas about how to search for biological parents. Jean Strauss' *Birthright: The Guide to Search and Reunion for Adoptees, Birthparents, and Adoptive Parents* (Penguin, 1994) and *Search: A Handbook for Adoptees and Birth Parents* (Onyx Press, 1998) are both excellent accounts of the means by which adult adoptees found their birth parents. These books detail the organizations that can help you, as well as the states with the most open documents.

To actually get a copy of your state's adoption laws, contact:

National Adoption Information Clearinghouse
P. O. Box 1182
Washington, DC 20013
naic@calib.com
http://www.calib.com/naic/

Agencies can certainly help your quest. One is the Adoptees' Liberty Movement Association (ALMA). National and local members share information with each other, including methods for gaining access to documents. They can be reached at:

ALMA
P. O. Box 727
Radio City Station
New York, NY 10101-0727
http://almanet.com/ ("genealogy resources")

You can also view the Adoptees web page (http://www.adoptees.com/) and sign up for its discussion group.

listserv@sjuvm.stjohns.edu
In the message, write: subscribe your first name your last name

Another discussion group is "Adopting":
majordomo@userhome.com
In the message, write: Subscribe adopting

The Orphan Train Heritage Society of America also has members who keep records on an early adoption movement known as the Orphan Train Movement, in which the Children's Aid Society of New York moved more than one hundred thousand street children to homes in the western states. This movement took place between 1850 and 1930, and many of the children were immigrants who had lost their parents during the voyage to America or shortly after arriving. If you think you or your ancestors were part of the Orphan Train Movement, write to:

> The Orphan Train Heritage Society of America
> 4912 Trout Farm Road
> Springdale, AR 72762

AFRICAN AMERICANS

Few records exist before 1865 concerning individual slaves. However, if you are willing to search, some sources do exist. Study local newspapers, which printed slave sale notices and runaway slave alerts with lengthy descriptions. Also, peruse the membership rolls of Southern churches. Even those with a mostly white membership often listed black members.

Courthouse deed records and bills of sale can identify slaves, typically by first name, age, and often occupation-if you know one of the parties involved in the transaction. But courthouses will probably not have documentation on vital events, because these typically were not officially recorded. Some of this information, however, can be found in works by The Writers Project of the Works Progress Administration. Writers for this project interviewed former slaves and produced forty-one volumes of stories. These were published in 1941 and reprinted in 1972 as *The American Slave: A Composite Autobiography* by Greenwood Publishing.

If your ancestor had the good fortune to be a "freedman," look to typical genealogical resources (especially city directories) and manumission (freed slave) records on file, affidavits of free persons, and registration of every person moving into a new county. The National Archives also has 98 microfilm rolls entitled *Volunteer Union Soldiers Who Served with the U.S. Colored Troops* arranged by surname.

Black-only papers, such as *National Era* (1847–1860), contain genealogical information as well. Know that between 1840 and 1860 about 50,000 slaves used the Underground Railroad to escape slavery and went to the northern states and Canada. Also, 15,000 freedmen left the United States to return to Africa between 1821 and 1860 and searchable databases exist on those names. (See http://www.ccharity.com/ for this database, which also included slave entries in wills, fugitive slave cases, manumission, etc.).

Following slave emancipation, the government set up the Bureau of Refugees, Freedmen, and Abandoned Lands to help former slaves until 1872. Its many records are in the National Archives along with another good source, records of the Freedmen's Savings and Trust Company, which had 29 branches.

Census reports also can be helpful. Free heads of households, including white males and females, and "all other free persons" (i.e., blacks) were listed in 1790–1810. Censuses from 1820–1840 listed free blacks by age groups; slaves were only mentioned as a total number within each slaveowner's household. The next two censuses list all persons in free households by name, and slaves by age and sex (but no name). The census from 1870 onward lists black family information just as it did for white families. Often former slaves took the surname of their previous owner, which can be confusing or helpful, depending on the individual situation.

For more detailed information, see the many fine books on this subject and the Ancestry web site (http://ancestry.com) for its on-line chapter 15, "Tracking African American Family History," from the 1997 print version of *The Source*, the genealogical classic. Also contact the Afro-American Historical and Genealogical Society, P. O. Box 73086, Washington, DC 20056-3086, and see the discussion group *Afrigeneas*, a mailing list created to promote African family history. To subscribe, send the message "subscribe afrigeneas" to majordomo@msstate.edu

HISPANIC AMERICANS

Most Hispanic Americans, true, have roots that lead to Spain. An important fact to remember is that just as the United States has been a melting point of countries, so has Central America, South America, and many Caribbean islands. So, when tracing roots, don't assume that all roads lead to Spain. You also may find Native American, German, Eastern European, Italian, African, and Portuguese ancestors! For relatives who came directly from Spain to the United States, look for passenger lists, particularly in Florida, Texas, and California, and special lists, such as the National Archives *List of Spanish Citizens Entering the Port of New Orleans Between 1840–1865*. For more information, read individual country listings in the previous chapter.

JEWISH AMERICANS

Almost all Jewish Americans are either Ashkenazic Jews (from France, Germany, and today's Austria, Czech Republic, Slovakia, Hungary, and Romania) or Sephardic Jews (from Spain, then expelled in 1492 and relocated to Holland or the Mediterranean). Before 1838, Jewish emigration to the United States was small. In the following 50 years, a wave of German migration occurred, which was followed from 1880–1924 by two million Eastern European Jewish emigrants. The Holocaust caused many Jews to migrate, and recent years have seen a great number of Russian Jews coming to the United States.

The hardest group to research are the Jews who came from Germany, because German genealogical research itself is so difficult. Those descended from Eastern European Jews have an easier search, because much information exists about this group, and the U.S. Government documented incoming immigration thoroughly during the 1890s. In 1906, in addition to town of last residence, occupation, and other information, place of birth was added. This information is available in the National Archives and its branches and the Family History Libraries. Naturalization papers will also be valuable sources, because most Jewish immigrants became Untied States citizens.

The majority of Jewish Americans descending from Ashkenazic Jews did not use surnames before the nineteenth century. Because of this practice, tracing lineage is usually limited to no more than two hundred years ago. During the Holocaust, half of all European

Jews were killed. Those who survived remembered their relatives and former lives in *yizkor* books that commemorate the towns from which they came. More than a thousand of these books have been produced and include information about families who survived and those who did not. The final section in these books lists those who did not survive. Avotaynu (see below) publishes a listing of these *yizkor* books and towns. Another source are "pages of testimony" documented by Yad Vashem, P. O. Box 3477, 91034 Jerusalem, Israel. Vashem has worked since 1955 to document the 6 million Jews killed in the Holocaust, and currently has records of half of them.

The publisher Avotaynu (http://www.avotaynu. com) is a leading publisher of Jewish genealogy products. It also has an Internet database of Holocaust-era Jews who had accounts in Swiss banks or assets held by the Austrian government. Not only does the site list the names, it also describes how to place a claim for the unclaimed assets. Avotaynu also hosts a Jewish genealogical trip to the Family History Library in Salt Lake City headed by veteran Jewish genealogists. Other web sites are JewishGen (http://www.jewish-gen.org) with hundreds of links is Jewish Genealogy Links (http://www.pitt.edu/~meisel/jewish) that lists archives, books, news groups, databases, family pages, surname dictionaries, and more!

Also contact the Jewish Genealogical Society (P. O. Box 6398, New York, NY 10128) for information and ask about local branches in your area.

NATIVE AMERICANS

Even though Native Americans have a long history in the United States, their individual recorded history is short. Until the mid-1800s, records listed only an individual man in relation to treaties and other documents. Those Indians who have long identification with a tribal group will have an easier search than the person who has only the family tradition of an Indian ancestor, but little other details.

Before starting, try to find the time period, tribe, and geographical area where your Native American ancestor lived. Each area and tribe has its own resources. Some, such as a few tribes in Texas, date to the mid-1700s. This is complicated by the many intermarriages that took place and oft-practiced common-law arrangements.

Pay close attention to census records. Often, Indians were recorded as general members of the population. In others, they may be listed as "colored" or have their last name be listed as "Indian." The 1870 census was the first to have a classification for Indians. Later censuses counted Indians on reservations.

In 1824, The War Department established The Office of Indian Affairs, which generated numerous records. Many of these records are stored at the National Archives. Its branches also have specialized collections, such as the Kansas City branch with Sioux and Chippewa records. The Fort Worth branch has the largest collection. When searching for records, look for:

- Indian Census Rolls, 1885–1940

- Removal records, 1815–1850

- Tribal enrollment records, 1827–present

- 1832 Census of the Creek Nation

- 1835 Census of the Cherokee Nation

- Land allotment records, 1856–1935

- Probate records, 1906–present

- Annuity rolls, 1850–1887

Searching the World Wide Web first may save you lots of time, because many Native American genealogy sites are on-line, such as *Native American Genealogy* (http://hometown.aol.com/bbbenge/front.html)

WOMEN

Law and custom have caused many women of the past to be known (if at all) by only their first name. This is because men ran most businesses, family property was held in the name of their husband or sons (at least until 1850), the children of a wife bore her husband's surname, and other reasons.

Often hidden in public records, a "feme covert," (a married woman) had far fewer rights than a "feme sole" (singled, widowed, or divorced woman). This, of course, varied by state and time period.

To get past these obstacles, look for collateral lines. That means the siblings of the woman. These names are on censuses, passenger lists, and the gravestones by the woman for whom you are searching. Collateral lines also surface when the court appoints a guardian for her children if her husband dies and in the middle names of the woman's children, because often a child has the middle name that was the mother's maiden name.

Some censuses may point the way, such as the 1925 Iowa census that identifies the maiden names of women. Censuses that list the birth place for each parent (e.g., 1880, 1900, 1910, and 1920) may also provide a clue if they use the age and first name of the woman. Death certificates, too, list birth places. Don't make assumptions when working with these few clues; find other supporting documentation.

Widows of soldiers in the Revolutionary War, War of 1812, and Civil War who made pension claims often gave their maiden names when presenting information for the claim. These records are stored at the National Archives and require form NATF to process. Obituaries and wedding notices, too, can give information ("nee Clarice Bohnsack" or "daughter of Bridget and Patrick Kirby").

Legal documents that require extensive documentation may provide you with the details you need. Emigration documentation might also show maiden names. Recommended books for further study are *The Hidden Half of the Family: A Sourcebook for Women's Genealogy* (Christina Kassabian Schaefer, Genealogical Publishing, 1999) and *A Genealogist's Guide to Discovering Your Female Ancestors* (Sharon DeBartolo Carmack, Betterway Books, 1998).

Chapter Twelve

WRITING YOUR FAMILY HISTORY

*L*earning about those who came before us is an adventure and the piecing together of a never-ending puzzle. For genealogical researchers, each new ancestor is a gem in their treasure chest of facts. But there comes a time when the hunt winds down. No new leads. Your stacks of genealogy notes and records are starting to overwhelm and confuse even yourself. Family members and friends keep asking, "Have you finished yet?"

If filling in genealogical charts satisfies you, and you plan on only being a data source, fine. However, sheet after sheet of vital statistics doesn't interest most family members. Nor does wading through a complex presentation of multiple family branches in an avalanche of dates, names, and footnotes. So, if you want to make your information accessible to others, you must write your research in a way they can understand it.

By relating genealogy in a narrative form, that is, a descriptive story rather than a series of charts, you will actually "write" history and tell a story that gives your reader something to remember. While you sift, sort, and arrange data, you will make discoveries that will add to the relevance of your genealogical research. Pick through your facts and use the ones that bring the story home. That does not mean you will leave out detailed information. You can present related and in-depth information in the appropriate place, such as an appendix or separate section.

As you make the leap from charts to narrative, that's where you, the historiographer, appear. Historiographers ("writers of history") make history readable. Good ones make history understandable. Great ones make it memorable.

Now, don't go on about how you need to do just a little more research before you start. Keep on researching . . . that's fine—just do that research while you write. Actually, writing can even help your research, because the act of writing makes you think, see gaps (yes! more research!), and put together information in new ways.

You don't have to be a wizard at composition. You just need a commitment to see this project through.

GETTING STARTED

Where to start on this writing quest? Which person goes where? What type of history should you write? Formal? Casual? Should you only include direct descendants of an immigrant ancestor? Or should you include all of the distant relatives, especially with a lot of information about people still living? Before you put too much effort into thinking of your answer, think of any family histories that impressed you.

Decide what "person" (otherwise known as *point of view*) in which you are going to be writing. Should you refer to yourself when writing? Some do, some don't. The twentieth century historical trend tends to use the editorial "we." Many historical authors also use the third person point of view ("He went to school") and refer to themselves as "the writer." To some, this stance projects modesty and appears objective.

Other experts think that referring to yourself as "I" (that's termed "first person," e.g., "I went to school") adds the charm of your own voice and is especially effective in oral histories because it energizes and authenticates the narrative. A variation on this is to use "I" in footnotes and in the introduction. Wrote Martin Duberman: "When a historian allows more of himself to show his feelings, fantasies, and needs—not merely his skills at information retrieval, organization, and analysis—he is less likely to contaminate the data simply because there is less pretense that it and he are one." Note: You are stepping out of the story when you include your personal comments; take care not to be disruptive.

How to Present Your Information

The next step is deciding how to present your information. Ask yourself: Who is my target audience? That is, who do you want to read this information. Only yourself? Immediate family? Parents, siblings, fourth cousins, future great-great-grandchildren? Genealogists? Knowing your intended audience is pivotal.

Determine exactly which relatives are to be included in this book. Mother's family? Dad's side? Both? How many generations and surnames? Cousins—second, third, fourth, etc.—too? Only living relatives? What about spouses' lines? What information will accompany each relative besides the usual birth, education, marriage, children, occupation, and death recordings? With whom do you start the story? Should you do more than one book? You have a vast amount of information, much of which needs to be effectively sorted for reader comprehension.

Look at the following ways and see whether one of these might work for your project.

1. The typical organization method in family histories is "chronological"—a progression of events in time. If you start with yourself or immediate family and work your way back, you are writing an "ascending" family history. The most popular chronological method (because it is the easiest) is to only include male descendants that carry the family surname.

Strict genealogists often follow the New England Register System of presentation, which originated in the magazine of the same name. Here each family is presented with the male designated family head. His descent to the common ancestor is noted, as are the personal data of himself and wife. Children are listed (with their personal data) in smaller type, tabbed right.

1—John JONES (1805–1879), Clermont, Ohio
sp—Catherine CAMERER (1805–1861)

2—Henry C. JONES (1831–1913)
sp—Dolly E. MIDKIFF (1834–1901)

3—Thomas R. JONES (1856–1880), Hancock, Indiana

It is a "descending" history if you start with a long-ago relative (the first known relative in the country is termed the "progenitor") and work toward the present. If you do a descending history, you might start with Abidiah and Sarah Lindley in your first chapter, then give each of their six children their own chapter. New chapters could be devoted to the families of each of the six children.

The following is a chronological descendance starting with the first known relative (Frederick Goss). "Christina Marries William" introduces a new family line as the descendance continues.

From Germany to North Carolina

"Major" Frederick

Frederick of the Flat Swamp

Sarah Comes to Missouri

Christina Marries William

The Itinerant Methodist Preacher

Jacob and His Brothers

The Spillers

John the "Entrepreneur"

Warren, the Story-Teller

Within each chapter, you can further sort information with sub-heads, which introduce text sections. For instance, in the chapter "From Germany to North Carolina," four subheads are possible:

The Ancestral Home

Frederick Flees to Switzerland

The Family Crosses the Atlantic

Homesteading by Fair Grove

2. The "parent-child-parent" method begins with the paternal grandfather, then paternal grandmother, and their life together. Then, introduce their child—your father—and his marriage with your mother. Then discuss maternal grandfather, maternal grandmother, and their life together. This method can start in the 1700s with a paternal grandparent and work its way to the present. Differentiate between generations with headings, such as "Ivan and Mary" or "Samuel the Entrepreneur and Ellen the Beauty."

3. You can use "divisions" (e.g., chapters) to group topics. Chapters can focus on individuals (Chapter 1: Abidiah Lindley; Chapter 2: Sarah Snow), a

whole family line (Chapter 1: The Pipkin Family: Chapter 2: The Snow Family), by generations, (Chapter 1: Abadiah and Sarah Lindley, Chapter 2: Kenneth and Elizabeth Lindley Harris) or other divisions (e.g., Family Legends, Family Weddings). One option is to start with an individual and his descendants in the first section, then discuss allied families in the next section, and end with U.S. and country of origin lineages. Geographical sorting might work best for some families. Do chapters by states (the Illinois Lindleys, Virginia Lindleys, etc.) by regions (the Lindleys in the South, Lindleys in the Upper Midwest), or by country (the Scottish Lindleys, the Irish Lindleys, the U.S. Lindleys).

4. Another type of arrangement is the "letter story." In *Warriors for the Working Day*, a 105-page book of letters written between two families during the Civil War, the author accompanies text with explanations, individual biographies, and historical overviews. Not many of us have the rare fortune to posses vintage letters, but we can use a similar technique. Writing letters to imaginary readers is similar to the detective hunt, because you are taking your reader along your solution path. This is a great way to write as you research. Theoretically, by the end of your research, you have written your story! A good idea is to write about a specific person or family in each fictional letter.

5. A twist on the letter idea is separating each chapter or individual with "outside information" that relates to the chapter topic. In the novel *How to Make an American Quilt*, Whitney Otto links the lives of eight women in a quilting group through quilt-related topics. The author introduces each woman's story with a short chapter of quilting instructions that are a metaphor for the next woman introduced. For instance, the chapter on war-time quilting precedes the story of a woman who had a son killed in Vietnam. In another, the author talks of preserving quilts before the story of a woman trying to preserve her marriage. You could do the same thing with recipes or other topics.

6. Photographs might inspire some reluctant writers. Arrange photos in the order you like, then write an explanation to go with each one. Go beyond a caption ("Millie Snow, 1933, Hampton Beach") and instead offer a detailed explanation ("The third daughter of Samuel and Hazel Snow was Millie, a fun-loving girl who loved the outdoors. Here, you see Millie on Hampton Beach at age 23, months before she married Walter Thomason, a conservation engineer from New Jersey.) On this same theme, you could arrange contents by maps, i.e., Chapter 1: Map of France; Chapter Two: Map of ancient Windsor, Connecticut; and so forth. For some, a videotape may be the best method of presentation for your information and audience. Have family members discuss other family members, do a walk-through of your house,

focusing on specific items and their family background, or a collage of a family reunion, individuals, home sites, etc.

7. If most of your information comes from tape-recorded interviews, use the power of your subjects' own words. After judiciously editing, your subject's own extended stories tell your family history. Interject explanatory text when necessary. One popular format is the question-and-answer format favored by today's magazine journalists:

The following is from a July 16, 1974 interview with Carlos Martinez.

Q: Why did you come to America?
A: My business was destroyed. My home burnt to the ground. I went first to Miami, then later to the north.

Q: How was the crossing?
A: The crossing was rough. Many were sick and brought with them few possessions.

You can take this same information and develop a lengthy introduction, then present the information with questions. Or pull out the best quotations and link them with explanations.

8. Arrange family members alphabetically. Each is a self-contained unit, including reference sources, with their genealogical chart position listed directly under the title.

9. The "detective hunt" lends itself well to genealogical publishing. In the book *Search for Father*, the author describes his extensive genealogical tracings and search for family letters and diaries before he solves a puzzle pertaining to his father. Because genealogists enjoy the thrill of tracking ancestories, this type of writing may be the best way to get the writing process started. Use this in your introduction, or, better yet, write an article of how you traced a relative, discovered ancestors in common, lucked into a ten generation genealogy written by a relative, actually touched records written by a great-great-great grandfather . . . Submit the article to a genealogical newsletter, your local newspaper, or even use it for your annual Christmas letter to the relatives!

If you are uncertain, look at other family histories before you begin writing. Most libraries have family histories. While you are at the library, look up back copies of *Everton's Genealogical Helper*. Near the end of every issue are family history reviews.

Chapter Thirteen

INCORPORATING THE ART OF STORYTELLING INTO YOUR FAMILY HISTORY WRITING

What does the art of storytelling have to do with recording family history? A lot!

Early storytellers told of heroes, sacred beings, man's origins, and the lineages of rulers who financially supported them. These first historians knew how to hold listeners' attention with suspense, humor, sound effects, and other compelling techniques.

Storytellers today may be the next-door neighbor with her racy tale about the school superintendent, or the television news anchor describing a courageous rescue. Both are accounts of factual happenings told in a manner that catches and retains listener attention.

Historical storytelling is not make-believe, nor is it history rewritten. Think about the dinosaurs in pictures and at museums. They are reconstructions, as is your family history, that have been pieced together from skeletal remnants.

Storytelling Techniques

The first trait a successful narrator has is enthusiasm. If something is exciting, let the readers know. Use exclamation points or your own opinion to let the reader know the reason for your excitement.

Storytellers also . . . pause. With a simple pause here and there, they heighten interest with suspense They allow the reader time to let words sink in. By shifting rhythm and pacing, they give listeners a break. Pause in your own writing by introducing history, philosophy, a song refrain, a photograph. You can also pause with punctuation marks such as the hyphen (-) or ellipsis (. . .). Keeping paragraphs short and varying sentence length also gives readers a break.

Repetition, also in the storyteller's bag of tricks, is a device used to hammer home a point and build up to a finale. The following paragraph repeats the word "He" as the sentence opener and the things this person "could not" do to climax the bring-it-on home, paragraph finale.

> He could not vote. He could not hold public office. He could not enter the army, nor any other military branch. And, perhaps, the most unfair of all, he could not attend the town church, the one in which he was baptized.

Storytellers love to surprise their audiences, too. Paul Aurandt, son of radio commentator Paul Harvey, who wrote the above example and who writes the script for his father's radio broadcast—*The Rest of the Story*—has perfected the surprise ending that makes Harvey's show so popular. You can use this technique when introducing famous relatives, residences now vastly changed ("and the land that was once Joseph Wilhoit's corn patch is now the main campus of the University of Illinois"), and the like by mentioning how a relative's life influenced history, or telling of other life twists.

A good story depends on what you include and what you leave out, that's why of all the devices used by storytellers, the most important is keeping a story clutter-free. That's no easy task. All writers strive to keep their readers turning pages, but also hate to part with the abundance of detail they have worked so hard to get.

But what about those details you can't fit into the story? Don't worry. You can use them in the appendix, footnotes, sidebars, or on family sheets. That way, those who desire a more involved accounting can access your treasure chest of hard-gained facts.

Remember to keep stories on target and clear. You may have to reduce the number of dates and leave out some distant relatives. That's okay! And don't fret whether your writing is "good enough" just because it sounds conversational. It is.

WRITING ABOUT PEOPLE ALIVE TODAY

When writing about relatives alive today you have so much information that it makes sifting through data to avoid clutter much tougher. Say we want to write about three siblings ages 64–72, each alive today. The oldest's career as a petrologist took him to sites all over the world. However, his hobby of collecting guns since age nine is one the first things to come to mind when thinking of him. A yellowed newspaper article of his early collection is relevant today:

> John Pipkin knows guns-lock, stock, and barrel. Already considered an expert, he hopes some day to become the world's greatest authority on arms. At his home, John has a collection of hundreds of bullets, guns, pistols, and other weapons. His library contains every technical book and magazine on the subject. He can tell the make, model, and caliber of many guns just by seeing the pictures.

That was written when John was age 16; now, he is 70, and you can imagine his collection. His brother William has two interests: A law career and overseeing his ranch. In fact, the local newspaper wrote a business news profile on William that happily he liked and even sent copies to various relatives. As for the last sibling, Jane, she held a variety of jobs before she had three children and left the work force. Jane does not have hobbies or collections as John, but she is proud of her college sorority and is active in a community organization. In writing about the three siblings, the facts we would emphasize would be hobbies, jobs, and group memberships. They have stood the test of time. We don't think it adds much to their profiles to write that John likes chocolate milk shakes, a certain television show, and the color red. But we do think it is relevant that John has a museum quality gun collection, including three canons, and a gun from the 1812 War.

WRITING ABOUT ANCESTORS

Those who work from life have an obvious advantage over writers who rely solely on documents to write family history. In most cases, the further back you go, the less you know about a relative. You could probably write a full-length treatise on your mother, but only a page about your great-grandmother.

Never say never! If you can come up with even just one interesting incident, you will be amazed at how a scrap of information, even the vaguest of memories, can brighten your story, especially if your accounting is heavy with dates.

Davida Easton, b. 1801 in Tennessee, was the mother of their 11 children: Martha (b. March 28,

1821, Ky.); Miranda (b. April 30, 1822, Ky.); John (b. Nov. 12, 1824, Ky.); Absolom (b. July 3, 1827, Ky.); David J. (b. 1832, Ky.); Franklin (b. Dec. 5, 1834, Ky.); Amelia (b. April 23, 1836, Ky.); Annalise (b. Jan. 18, 1838, Mo.); Rawley (b. May 11, 1840, Mo.); Carolina (b. Feb. 27, 1843, Mo.); and Jesse (b. Feb. 16, 1847, Ar.).

They sat outside their cabin in the evenings and watched Indians traveling to the trading post at Pigeon Grove. One day an Indian (Osage, maybe) came to their cabin asking for a chicken to eat. Davida said he could have the chicken, providing he shot off the chicken's head with an arrow. The Indian did just that and left with his headless chicken.

August (d. 1882) and David (d. 1875) are buried in Pine Creek Baptist Cemetery. Their son Franklin married Elizabeth Fulks who died March 11, 1860 at age 30 leaving four children: Frances (b. April 2, 1854, Ks.), Amanda (Jan. 15, 1856). . . .

See how that anecdote about the Indian and chicken in the second paragraph helps separate the sea of dates? Even if you think an anecdote is corny, irrelevant, or even dubious, think twice about omitting a story tidbit that might turn out to be your audience's favorite.

BREAK INTO SONG

A song lightens the load. As you tell about your relative's mid-nineteenth century journey across the plains, throw in a song from that era:

Sweet Betsy From Pike

Oh, don't you remember sweet Betsy from Pike?
She crossed the wide prairie with her husband Ike.
With two yoke of oxen, an old yellow dog,
and a fat Shang-hai rooster and one spotted dog.

Place a hymn with a death account, a rocking song from the 1950s for a high school graduation, and so on. Add these touches after you have written your narrative.

ADDING PERSONALITY

"But all I know about this person are dates and locations. I don't have any anecdotes. I don't know anything else."

Maybe you do.

Think back to Chapter Four when we encouraged you to talk with relatives and look at old belongings. Do you have any books belonging to your subject. The type of book alone will give perspective on your individual. Biographies? Romance Novels? Non-fiction? Look inside. Is anything underlined? Scribbled in the margins? One family history writer found this poem in the Bible of her ancestor born in 1871:

Keep your troubles to yourself
Put them on the upper shelf;
Far away as it may be,
Where no eye but God's can see.
Give of treasures you possess,
Loving care and tenderness,
Cheerful smiles or sordid self,
But keep your troubles to yourself.

Inspirational words that this woman may or may not have lived by (bet she did!), but a practice she found commendable. This short poem gives a sense of her personality, doesn't it?

How about signatures? Besides being great for illustration purposes, signatures may shed light on your subject's personality. The quality of the handwriting can suggest the person's experience with writing, state of health, and other factors.

Perhaps you have something the person made. A quilt? A sampler? A chair? Add information about that piece to your writing. Lucky writers may even have a will of their ancestor listing household contents, properties, and the meaning-packed section on what each relative inherited.

INSERT YOURSELF

This is your version of the family history. How did you feel about what your great-great uncle did? What proverb did that incident in 1791 remind you of? Put in your opinion!

Adventurous story writers might enjoy inserting imaginative speculation in their work. One local author used this technique in her book about an historic building and the people who owned it. She began the account by interviewing the building. Yes, that's exactly what she did, and while that might not be our style, her approach may work wonderfully for your history. You could do something similar with a family house, farm, or business. Use this method as an introduction, ending, or sprinkle imagination throughout.

Also feel free to interweave the present. Include your own observations about a sight that once was and how it appears now.

> Route 672 crosses the North Shenandoah River on a concrete causeway type bridge. Obviously, it is intended to be flooded during high water. Looking upstream, I saw a suspension foot-bridge high above the water. This must be for foot access during high water. The foot bridge comes out behind, what I would believe to be, Jacob Frances' original settlement site.

If you don't want to include yourself or can't get to the exact location, include geographical information about that area to give readers an idea of the place in which your ancestors lived. To get the information, look at state tourism brochures, books on the state itself, and other publications. These resources will also describe typical crops grown in the area, which may be the same as those grown a hundred years ago. Agricultural information can also be obtained at county extensions and state agricultural reports that contain information about manufacturing and land quality.

FROM START TO FINISH OR . . . ?

Family members are the characters in your family history. You can start discussing your relative at his or her birth and do a step-by-step progression through time, but you don't have to. We first learn about many people at various times in their lives, not necessarily birth. In "Hail to Mom," a *People* Magazine profile of President Bill Clinton's mother Virginia Kelley, the author begins by telling a story about Bill Clinton. The anecdote is followed with:

> "They say the apple doesn't fall far from the tree, and in the case of America's President-elect, and his mother, the proverb holds. If you want to know where Clinton first learned to use his head—not to mention where he got his informidable take-a-licking-and-keep-on-ticking spirit—look no further than Virginia Cassidy Blythe Clinton Dwirre Kelley. In her 60 years, Kelley, a former nurse-anesthetist, has survived the deaths of three husband (one of them an abusive alcoholic), suffered the heartbreak of having her younger son Roger jailed for dealing cocaine, battled breast cancer, and during her son Bill's campaign, endured disturbing scrutiny."

In the next paragraph, Clinton discusses his mother's spirit and the author gives a description of her home, followed by a typical day. Then, in the fifth paragraph, the chronological story of Kelley unfolds, beginning with "Virginia Cassidy was born twelve miles from Hope, Bill Clinton's birthplace, in Bodcaw, Arkansas, in 1923. As you can see, in this introduction the author gave us:

- A story that the featured character told

- A summary of life challenges

- A quote

- A description of the subject's home

- A day in her life

- The cradle-to-grave story

This is not a novel organization. Biographical writers move around in time and commonly introduce characters at a high or pivotal point in their subject's lives. Read biographies to get an idea of well-written personal history!

ENDINGS

Just as beginnings don't have to start with births, neither do endings have to close with death.

Endings offer a good place to say "I wonder" ("I wonder: In the end, did he lose his brogue and speak in the flat upstate twang?") and muse. Endings also can hearken back to a previous part of the story, often the beginning (". . . and the rose bush that she brought from her parents' home was ablaze with blossoms") and tell the effect an individual had on others ("One of his descendants became a U.S. senator; a list of her descendants covers fifteen, single-spaced pages").

And, as we end here, remember that recording your family's history has been challenging and exhilarating. However, if you want family members to read your work, consider incorporating story-telling devices to attract and keep your readers' attention.

Who knows? You might end up like Janice Woods Windle who, while compiling a family cookbook for her oldest son, decided to write a one-page summary of her relatives' lives to accompany the recipes. One decade and 451 pages later, her modest project turned into *True Women*, a sweeping novel of Texas' past that covered six generations of Windle's family from Texas' war of independence to World War II!

Chapter Fourteen

USING HISTORY IN FAMILY HISTORY WRITING

$\mathcal{B}$esides making your family story more interesting, interjecting history into your work gives readers insight and understanding. How many people today know the changing boundaries of Germany through time? Not many. What was cholera? If that was the reason for a relative's death, your readers will appreciate learning about this past threat. Providing explanatory historical information also makes your work more responsible. If you write that Sarah Huff lived in a sod house, you should explain to your readers how a sod house was built and why this form of housing was used.

HISTORY ADDS CLARIFICATION

Perhaps you are writing about long-ago ancestor and know only a surname, occupation, or other tidbits. How can you add to that meager offering? History! By providing historical description, you give a fuller picture of your ancestor's lives. For instance, present the known facts:

> Sarah, with the help of at least one slave, purchased a claim near the west line of Webster County. This first homesite consisted of a log cabin with a puncheon floor and a few acres of plowed ground.

From a county history written in the nineteenth century, we read about early life in Webster County where Sarah lived and adds to the preceding paragraph:

> A log house could be erected in one day if a few men with sharp axes pooled their talents. These sturdy cabins had one to two rooms with a loft for sleeping. Fireplaces were made of huge stones. Some settlers built fireplaces with sticks coated with mud, an unsafe, but common building practice. For flooring, settlers used packed dirt, or had "puncheon" floors, similar to Sarah. The latter flooring consisted of rough hewn logs laid parallel to each other about three feet apart. Additional

boards fastened down with wooden pins overlaid the lower boards.

By adding this information, we provided more understanding of Sarah's life and explained what a puncheon floor was. Readers want your writing to make sense. For instance, many people have the rare fortune to possess ancestor's letters, diaries, or other personal writings. Those items can be printed as is, of course, but they don't always make sense by themselves. By providing additional details to these personal writings and their unfolding story, you will help hold your reader's attention.

Take the example of one diary, which consisted of numerous single-line entries. One entry was simply: "We was about tuckered." Not too interesting. But when the writer explains next to the entry that the diarist and his regiment had marched more than 20 miles a day to be on time for an upcoming Civil War battle, which the author then elaborates on using outside sources, that brief, understated entry becomes more poignant.

One writer was one of the lucky ones who had an ancestor's 1863 journal written on the Oregon Trail. While some daily entries stood out, many were hard to understand because of spelling and sketchy information. By itself, she knew few would give this journal the attention it deserved. So, she got a couple of books and maps of the Oregon Trail and matched up ancestor Eli's stops with points along the trail. She then wrote a general overview of the Oregon Trail with specific focus categories from the journal.

For instance, in the category on "hunting," she found 11 entries on animals that the trail travelers killed and ate: "Antelope proved to be the most predominant game Eli killed, and buffalo, although desired, were not to be found."

Problems that travelers had with various illnesses were detailed in the interesting category "illness and death": "Travelers frequently told of deaths on the road. Youngsters bounced out of wagons and were run over by wheels. Irate cattle attacked their care-takers. Firearms accidentally discharged in jolting wagons. Bad water caused illness. . . . " Specific examples from Eli's journal included, "On June 16, I wos takin viantly sick to my stomach & puked Like fury. Electta fixed me some Cayann peper tea & it Settled my Stomach."

HISTORY PROVIDES A SETTING

One of the best reasons to add history is to give readers a background for your story. Theatrical plays have a backdrop and scenery, and so should your family history! This added dimension also gives your readers a break from the blizzard of dates and name listings that many family histories end up being. Trying to follow avalanches of "who begat whom begat whoms" is tedious at best, confusing for sure. Give readers a break by inserting relevant historical background that relates to your story. Here's a short, bare-bones description:

Frederick Goss was born in 1701. He emigrated from his native Germany to Pennsylvania with four of his children (some of whom may have been born in Switzerland) and settled in Rowan County, North Carolina.

Now, before we go on and list those children and their offspring, we are going to insert a paragraph on North Carolina at the time Goss emigrated.

By 1710, settlements in North Carolina had spread down the Carolina coast. Although pirates, especially Blackbeard, preyed on the settlers, by 1729, North Carolina had a population of 36,000, most still on the coast. That number would increase ten-fold by 1775 and spread westward across the Piedmont into the mountains.

Okay, that added paragraph may not be the most exciting of information, but it will help keep readers reading. Then we resume with our accounting of the Goss family.

HISTORY FLESHES OUT "BARE BONES" STORY AREAS

Ideally, you have about the same amount of information on each family member so that your book is balanced. Wouldn't that be nice! In reality, you may have a lot on one member or family side and almost nothing on another. Adding related history to these bare areas makes for more even reading and helps correct the balance.

HISTORY GIVES PIZZAZZ

Let's say you write about ancestor Felix, his parents, occupation, and brief settlement in Pennsylvania. You list his brothers (one a North Carolina senator), marry him off and settle him in Salisbury, North Carolina. Besides his death date and children's names, this is all you have. On to the next relative? Not just yet. Here's a tie-in that will catch readers' attention and give an elementary school child something to talk about at recess. Tell about Felix's famous neighbor, Daniel Boone and his ten siblings, who also lived along the Yadkin River by Salisbury. Add information from Boone's biographers, such as the plentiful deer for hunting and trading done in the local markets of Salisbury. You will have made a historical connection that readers will remember.

EASY HISTORY SOURCES

But, you say, I have already done all this family research, I don't want to have to wade through history books now. You don't have to. In most cases, you can easily get information.

Start by going to your local library and looking in the 940–990 Dewey Decimal Section for history publications. Ask your local historical society or museum about topics that pertain to your individual history. Another starting point is the encyclopedia, especially good for describing the environment or times in which your ancestor lived. If your ancestor sailed to Philadelphia in 1806, look up Pennsylvania, then target its history section.

Try world almanacs (they don't have to be current). Almanacs can provide information about populations of a particular time, state history, and summaries of religions (which can be very enlightening considering what a part religion can play in people's lives and our limited understanding of others' spiritual beliefs).

Local histories are invaluable. In local histories, you can find out about the wildlife, vegetation, soil, housing styles, entertainments, and more-all of which you can add to your story.

The Early American House: Household Life in America 1620–1850 is one such book. Chapters include early houses, chimneys, fireplaces, kitchenware, food, drink, and everyday life. Here, you will discover that copper and brass kettles were held in great esteem, iron kettles not. (Think that's unimportant? Think again! Wills from the eighteenth and nineteenth century commonly mention kettles, which if large, were valued as high as $400 dollars!) Be sure and look for "timeline" books that give information about particular years. Most of these deal with the twentieth century, such as *Time-Life's* compilations of various years. A short timeline is provided (*see Figure 7 on next page*) to give you an idea of world events since the recording of genealogy.

Software computer programs can also give you past snippets to interlace in your story. For instance, if you plug in the date for February 27, 1956 on one software program, the computer screen shows the events that happened that day and events of the year, such as the University of Alabama enrolled its first black student; President Eisenhower turned down a request by Israel to purchase military arms from the United States; Brink's $2.7 million robbery solved as FBI identified the seven men involved; Rocky Marciano retired as undefeated heavyweight champion of the world; Pat Flaherty won the Indy 500 averaging 128.5 mph; and New York beat Brooklyn in the World Series. The program also offers the cost of living, popular songs, and movies.

Other software programs can also be used to enliven your family history, such as Genelines (Progeny Software, Box 1600, 232 Main Street, Wolfville, NS BOP Ixo, Canada, 10800-565-0018, www.progenysoftware.com). This program has the capability to place your family in context of other historical events. It works with popular genealogical software to show life events for individuals and can trace family members over time showing when different family members were alive.

Figure 7: TIMELINE

1066: William the Conqueror wins English rule

1200: Incas began to build empire based in Peru

1300: The Renaissance begins in Europe and signals end of Middle Ages

1337: Hundred Years War begins between England and France

1347–1352: Plague epidemic called the Black Death kills up to three quarters of European and Asian population

1415: Portuguese begin to develop trade with West Africa

1434: Medici family begins domination of Florence and makes that city center of Italian Renaissance

1478: Start of Spanish Inquisition

1492–1504: Christopher Columbus makes four voyages to America

1497: John Cabot of England lands on eastern coast of Canada

1517: Martin Luther begins Protestant Reformation and inspires Peasants' War in Germany

1519–1521: Hernando Cortes conquers Aztec empire in Mexico

1562: French begin persecution of Huguenots, French Protestants

1565: Spaniards found St. Augustine in Florida, now the oldest city in United States

1581: Netherlands revolt against Spain and gain independence

1587: John Knox founds Presbyterian religion in Scotland

1550: Christianity introduced into Japan by St. Francis Xavier

1565: St. Augustine, Florida, first permanent settlement in United States

1595: Dutch began to colonize East Indies

1601: Portuguese, Spanish, and Dutch begin to visit Australia

1607: English found Jamestown in America, their first permanent settlement

1609: First newspapers appear in Europe

1618: Thirty Years War starts and creates conflict between Catholics and Protestants in Europe and devastates Germany

1620: Mayflower ship reaches Plymouth, Massachusetts

1627: Japan begins to exclude foreigners

1643–1715: Louis XIV (the Sun King) rules in France and art and culture flourish

1665: Great Plague hits London and following year a fire destroys the city

1680: Germans begin to colonize West Africa

1681: King of England gives present state of Pennsylvania to William Penn for a colony

1682–1725: Peter the Great tries to "westernize" Russia

1721: Latin Americans begin revolts to obtain independence from Spain

1738: John Wesley, founder of Methodism, begins to preach in England

1750: Industrial Revolution begins in England

1756: Start of Seven Years War in which France lost Canada to England

1760: 1.5 million people living in the 13 colonies of the United States

1768: Turkey and Russia begin century of wars

1775–1783: American Revolution

1789: French Revolution; George Washington becomes first U.S. president

1803: U.S. purchases Louisiana Territory from France

1807: Britain outlaws slave trade; France, Spain, and Portugal follow

1807: Robert Fulton invents steamboat

1810: Mexico fights for independence from Spain, obtains independence in 1821; the next year Brazil and Peru obtain independence

1819: U.S. purchases Florida from Spain

1821: Greeks begin move for independence from Turkey and become independent in 1830

1822: Liberia founded as haven for freed American slaves

1825: Bolivia becomes last Latin American country to gain independence from Spain

1831: Russia begins "Russification" of Poland

1837–1901: Reign of Queen Victoria in England

1839–1842: England acquires Hong Kong with victory in Opium War over China

1841: Dr. David Livingston begins exploration of central Africa and his reports create interest in the "Dark Continent"

1845: Potato blight begins in Ireland; one million dead from starvation and disease by 1851

1846: Mexican War with U.S. for Texas begins

1846: Elias Howe invents first practical sewing machine

1848: Gold discovered in California

1853: Japan agrees to trade with West

1854–1856: Britain and France end Russian domination of south-western Europe with victory in Crimean War

1861: Civil War begins at Fort Sumter

1867: Diamonds discovered in South Africa

1869: Suez Canal opens

1889: More than 20,000 settlers compete for land in Oklahoma Territory on April 22

1895: Marconi sends message over "wireless"

1905: Albert Einstein formulates theory of relativity

1910: Japan annexes Korea

1911: Chinese Revolution

1914: Assassination of Archduke Francis Ferdinand of Austria sparks World War I

1917: Bolshevik Revolution in Russia

1919: Prohibition enacted and later repealed

1921: Chinese Communist party founded

1928: Stalin initiates plan for rapid industrialization in Russia; those who refuse are either sent to Siberia for forced labor or killed; over five million peasants "liquidated"

1929: Stock market crash launches Great Depression in U.S.

1935: Congress passes a series of social security laws

1937–1945: Japan invades China

1939: Beginning of World War II

1945: U. S drops atomic bombs on Hiroshima and Nagasaki beginning Nuclear Age

1950: Beginning of Korean War (ends 1953)

1954: U.S. Supreme Court rules public school segregation of races is unconstitutional

1961: East Germany builds the Berlin Wall to prevent the escape of East Germans from Communism

1963: Start of the War in Vietnam, which generates protest demonstrations in late 1960s

1969: First man on the moon

1974: President Nixon resigns from office after Watergate scandal

1975: Soviet Union takes over Angola; Ethiopia in 1977

1977: Djibouti, the last European colony in Africa, is granted independence

1980: Ayotallah Kohmeini overthrows Shah of Iran

1982: First permanent artificial heart implanted in U.S.

1986: First official observation of Martin Luther King Day

1986: The rule of Ferdinand Marcos of the Philippines ends

1988: U.S. has worst drought in 50 years

1989: U.S. troops invade Panama

1990: President Bush signs Americans With Disabilities Act barring disability discrimination

1991: Persian Gulf War

1994: Republican party wins both houses in Congress

1997: First mammal cloning takes place in Scotland

1999: Stock market continues greatest bull run in history as world prepares to celebrate the new millennium

KNOW WHAT YOU ARE WRITING ABOUT

Including general history in your work adds dimension, reader relief, and entertainment. None of this will matter if your history is incorrect. How good are you on history? Take this little quiz and find out!

1. Which city was the busiest colonial port and largest manufacturing center of the mid-1700s?

2. Voting requirements differed in various colonies. What was the most important requirement needed to vote?

3. What was the colonists' basic food?

4. True or false? The health of colonists was poor by today's standards.

5. Which contagious epidemics took many colonial lives? Measles, smallpox, typhoid fever, bubonic plague. Yellow fever.

Answers: Philadelphia, Property ownership, Corn (eaten commonly as corn bread), True (but no worse than any other part of the world), Yes (all of these).

The point? You can't read too much history before you write your own history. And watch those assumptions!

Chapter Fifteen

INFORMATION PRESENTATION

DETERMINE YOUR ETHICAL STANCE

*B*efore you get too far in your writing, take time to objectively study your research and its presentation. As a historian, your job is to stick to the facts.

For instance, do not let kindliness color your judgment when evaluating information. Perhaps you write about a cousin who is illegitimate with no known biological father. The cousin's mother tells you to write down her new husband's name for the cousin's father. What should you do?

Or how about including your great-uncle's bankruptcy after an ill-advised financial speculation? It's the only fact you have about your great-uncle, but should he be immortalized on paper for this one misadventure—a failure that might have been his only trip-up in decades? Is it better not to write anything than write about this one fact that might present an unbalanced portrait of the real man? Should you include it because it's a fact and you don't have anything else? Or should you state that you know little else about this man except for the bankruptcy and include a personal comment that this same man might have been financially successful in his other decisions or maybe not, but this is all you know?

Along the same line, consider a man whose only living family member remembers that once the man, by then age 78 with signs of senility, forgot to put his pants on and walked down the street (pantless) to a wedding. Should he be remembered for age-related events of which he had no control? Is this fact relevant?

What about the family member who is a real pain in the neck? A loud-mouthed drunk? Or one self-destructive with chronic mental illness? These less than pleasant realities do stand out, but what do you whitewash, delete, or emphasize in your writing?

These are ethical questions for which you will have to come up with answers. Just try to avoid one-dimensionality—most people aren't one hundred percent heroes or villain. When making ethical decisions, cast emotions aside.

One last note: Don't eliminate an unpleasantry about your favorite aunt and emphasize the same trait for another relative you dislike. Be consistent and fair!

AVOID FAULTY REASONING

Logical pitfalls loom before you as you analyze information. While you write, ask "Am I overgeneralizing?

That is, am I drawing a conclusion from insufficient evidence?" If a man owns the largest house in town, is he the richest man in town? Not necessarily. He could have it mortgaged to the hilt. It could be collateral for a sinking business. Or it could be decorated with the barest of furnishings because all his money went to the house itself.

Ask "Am I oversimplifying?" That is, are you making a conclusion and ignoring part of your information? Saying that your great-grandmother was a saint on earth and loved by all is nice. But it is fallacious if you neglect to say that everyone liked her except for her mother-in-law, next-door neighbor, and the school board members to whom she wrote criticisms to on a weekly basis.

Are you assuming one event caused another because it followed in time? Time sequence does not prove cause and effect. Michael Woodward left his farm to fight in the Civil War. Because Woodward left, crops were half their normal averages. Was that because he was gone and his brother who farmed the land in his place was an inferior manager? What about droughts? Hail? Insect infestation? Broken equipment?

Beware of accuracy traps, and don't be too eager to draw a conclusion. When presenting your information, note dubious facts!

CONSIDER THE SOURCE

When separating fact from fiction, as journalism professors say, don't trust anyone, not even your mother. Feel free to make merry in situations of doubt, to use words such as "conflicting," "improbable," "illogical," "probably not," "unlikely," "could be," "possible," "apparently," "definitely," "positively," and other words denoting evaluation.

Look up any fact of which you are not sure. If the 1895 letter written by William Montgomery says that his family left France in the early sixteenth century because they were Huguenots—look up Huguenots in the encyclopedia. If you do, you will find that this Protestant group rose to favor during the reign of Henry II (1547–1559) and it was after that date that the Catholic government began persecuting this group. So, if your relative was a Huguenot, that relative left France later than William Montgomery's account. The point: Tell readers what William Montgomery wrote, but also let them know what other sources offer either in a separate explanation or with inserted brackets [ ], an easy way to introduce author notes.

PROVE IT! AND PROVE IT AGAIN! AND AGAIN!

If you have the proof, let the reader know for your own work's authenticity and also for their own hunt. Genealogy mistakes can happen and are repeated until someone makes a correction. As you review findings, ask "Have I proved this fact to my readers?" Remember the importance of primary sources—those records that happened at the time (e.g., a letter, newspaper article)—and secondary sources—publications written years after the fact (e.g., a biography).

DEFINITIONS

We are all guilty of imprecision in word usage. That is why you should look up questionable words in dictionaries, even words you think you know. For instance, what is a homestead? A general definition for homestead is a house and land. A more precise definition is a place of residence and small piece of land (one to five acres usually) reserved by law from creditors. It can also mean the 160 acres obtained free from the U.S. government under the Homestead Act of 1862 and subsequent land laws. If you have doubts, look up the word. If you don't have doubts, you should.

DOCUMENTATION

Providing evidence for historical conclusions reassures readers of your history's credibility. That doesn't mean you have to include document copies to authenticate your writing; although you may want to include part or all of a document for point emphasis, illustration (e.g., ornate marriage license), or explanation (handwriting example and why you deciphered it a certain way). If you want to include numerous documents, consider placing them in a special appendix at the back of the book for those readers who do want to examine information sources. Your writing should "prove" the facts in your narrative. Think of history books and text books. They provide the facts, but not the actual documents from which the facts were derived.

Besides giving your work credibility and authority, acknowledging sources provides readers information to locate sources for themselves. It's also good manners: Whenever you are indebted to a source for a quotation or a particular thought, acknowledge that source. If you don't, you are guilty of plagiarism (borrowing from another and presenting the information as your own work).

SOURCE CITATION

Informally, you may credit a source similar to these examples, "According to Aunt Bessie, Mamie had a big mouth," or in "Smith's 1884 *History of Brown County*, we find that Mamie Johnson ran a dry-goods store and was known for her love of gossip." Embedding source information, however, causes reader interruption and should be used sparingly. Therefore you have four options: in the acknowledgments section, in footnotes, in endnotes, or in the bibliography.

If you mention sources in your acknowledgments, you might write:

The majority of the information in this booklet came from a 15 October 1897 *Salina Chronicle* news article and *Salina City Directories from 1875–1900*. A 1902 family letter, now in the Spencer Collection at the University of Kansas, also provided information, as did interviews with Joy Clouse, Marlene Evinger, Rex Burkhardt, and Pat Johnston.

Family history books of a more formal nature require "reference" footnotes. You would put these footnotes at the bottom of each page on which they appear. Footnotes at each chapter end or the end of your work are termed "endnotes," which follow the same format, but are located on a separate page. You can put the reference source in numeral superscript as shown here:

- [1]Betty Jo Weaver Windel, *Yadon-Pennybaker Family History*, (Vinita, OK: Heritage Books, 1990), p. 27.
- [2]*Kansas City Star*, 5 June 1955.
- [3]Interview with Laurie Shea, Los Angeles, California, 12 May, 2000.

Or in brackets
- Jerimiah and Helen Tuttle were buried in the northeast corner of the family homestead [15].

and provide source information on another page

- [13] Personal interview with Fern Long, President of the Eudora Area Historical Society, 5 June, 1986
- [14] 1880 Federal Census; Lake County, Indiana; Eagle Creek Township
- [15] Family Bible now belonging to Nancy Gale, Rural Route, Centerville, Iowa.

The other type of footnote is the "content" footnote. It provides readers with extra information. You don't have to footnote the fact that Abraham Lincoln was our sixteenth president, but you should footnote lesser-known facts that might be unfamiliar to the reader. Content notes also provide translations. You might put the English translation in your book and provide the actual High German quote in your footnote. Use content footnotes to compare sources (e.g., birth certificate spells it "Minerva; 1942 signature reads "Menerva") and information not strictly pertinent to the immediate text. Perhaps you are writing about the tools your great-grandfather owned. In a content note you might describe the use of a particular tool. Or you might list your great-grandfather's tool inventory.

When citing footnote sources, follow a specific form, such as those in *Chicago Manual of Style*; *Turabian's Manual for Writers of Term Papers, Theses, and Dissertations*; the *MLA Handbook*, etc. The book long-hailed in genealogical circles is *Cite Your Sources: A Manual for Documenting Family Histories and Genealogical Records* (Polyanthos, 1980) by Richard Lackey. Elizabeth Mills' newer publication *Evidence: Citation & Analysis for the Family Historian* (Genealogical Publishing, 1997) is also recommended.

The basic listing for a publication written by one author is:

1) Author first name and surname

2) Book title

3) City book published in (and state if not clear by city alone):
Publisher, year published

4) Page number(s)
An example is:
Troy Lynch. *The Werst Family: 1680–2000* (Springfield, IL: Lynch Printing, 1998), p. 81.

Single space entries and divide them with double spacing. Place a comma after the author's name and city, printer, and year published in parentheses. For two authors, separate the full name of each author with "and."

William Crane and Nancy C. Crane

For periodicals (publications issued at intervals, e. g., newsletters and magazines), the format is:

1) Author first name and surname

2) Article title

3) Publication in which the article appeared

4) Issue date

5) Page number

An example would be:

Thomas Randall, "John Simmons, a Plantar," *Genealogical Helper*, (Dec. 1992), p. 33.

For an article without a known author, use the above format starting with the article title. Newspapers follow the same format except section and column number are often given:

Ashley Sokolof, "Local Civil War Skirmishes," *Emporia Gazette*, (Dec. 13, 1964), Sec. B, p. 4B, col. 2

On occasion you may cite a source more than once. In subsequent reference, you only need to include the author's last name, followed by the publication title, and page number:

Sokolof, *Emporia Gazette*, p. 4B.

When you are citing the same source as the one before it, you may use the common citation "ibid," a Latin abbreviation that means "in the same place." Ibid refers to the immediate preceding source and means that you are using the same source for the footnote:

Sokolof, *Emporia Gazette*, p. 4B
Ibid, p. 4B.

Another footnote you may use concerns personal interviews. Usually, this requires the name of the person interviewed and the date:

Personal interview with Glen Wineinger, 22 December 1945.

Adding the interview location is a nice touch!

If this seems confusing, you're right! That is why style manuals have pages of examples for citing sources and distinguish between reprints of earlier editions, anthology selections, unpublished dissertations, unsigned articles in encyclopedias, etc.

BIBLIOGRAPHIES

Footnotes credit each source. A bibliography is a listing of all the sources used in writing a book and is always found at the book end. Bibliographies can be very short or several pages long. Strict genealogists may say not to include a bibliography because all information in a family history should be specifically linked to each source. For those who feel that documenting each fact would make writing the family narrative too odious, then a bibliography is essential.

Typically, bibliographic entries include the same information found in footnotes (except they do not list page numbers), but differ in that the author's last name starts the citation, a period follows the title, and no parentheses are used.

Lynch, Troy. *The Werst Family: 1680–2000.* Springfield, IL: Lynch Printing, 1998.

Periodical example:
Randall, Thomas. "John Simmons, a Plantar," *Genealogical Helper.* Dec. 1992.

Personal interview:
Breithaupt, Elfrieda. Personal interview. 22 December 1945. Miami, Florida.

For hard-to-find books, it is helpful to tell where the book can be located. Many books that genealogists use are only at certain libraries in the country.

Chapter Sixteen

EDITING YOUR WRITING

When you think you have put down all your information in an organized and readable fashion, polish your text until it shines.

CONCEPT EDITING

The first polishing level is "concept editing" or "cut and paste" rewriting. Ask yourself: Is my information in the best sequence? Did I write too much about one relative and not enough about another? Should I move that paragraph that seems out of place on page fifteen? Even though it made sense when you first wrote it, on second look, you will see that some sections should be moved, some cut altogether, a few shortened to one sentence, and so forth. Computers make inserting, deleting, rearranging, and erasing easy; but you can do the same editing on type- or hand-written pages. Just be sure to leave ample space between lines. Write on one side of the page, too, in case you cut out paragraphs with scissors and paste them elsewhere in your work.

Since you are writing a readable history, offer information in small portions. If needed, summarize large chunks of information. You might be proud of a document that took a long time to track down, but do you need to reproduce it or type 15 paragraphs of legal verbiage to tell readers that Elizabeth Konig became a U.S. citizen in 1954? If you want to share this detailed information, put it in your appendix.

LINE EDITING

"Line editing" keeps sentences flowing and readers interested. Line editing cuts out wordiness, demystifies murkiness, and fills in sketchy sentences. One of the first line edits to check for are over-long sentences that make reading difficult. How can you tell whether a sentence is too long? Read it aloud. If you lose yourself or run out of breath, your sentence is too long. Another clue is a sentence with more than 25 words. Tighten sentences by eliminating words or revising one sentence into two. However, sentences don't all have to be short; that makes writing stilted. Vary sentence length to keep reader interest. For instance, if five consecutive sentences are short, combine two, so the writing isn't choppy.

Challenge yourself to cut thirty percent of your writing. It *can* be done and makes for better writing. To start, delete without mercy the word "the." Look over your writing and ask yourself if "the" in each case adds to the sentence. Does the sentence make sense without it?

Boonville Avenue, the site of Li's original residence. (Take out "the," you don't need it.)

Whittle away until only relevant information remains.

He emigrated to America to Pennsylvania. (Cut "to America")

Reduce prepositions, such as "of, to, for, on," because they often are only repeating information. Instead of "Born in the fall of 1827 on September 19, Scott Pringle. . . ," try "Born 19 Sept., 1827, Scott Pringle. . . ." Change "One of the sons was a gun-maker" to "One son was a gun-maker" or "One son, a gunmaker." Multiple prepositions confuse rather than clarify.

While you are at it, take out irrelevant qualifiers. You don't need "really," "very," "most," "relatively," "virtually," and others of that sort. The same goes for adjectives that repeat, but not add. "She lived in a small, 4-room house." Does "small" add to the sentence? (Four rooms is a small house.) Why not substitute color ("white"), material ("brick"), condition ("immaculate"), or another adjective?

Delete extra fluff with fervor, but, keep in mind, that you might need to put in new information. Insert words, sentences, or paragraphs for clarity, background, and unanswered questions. Use linking words liberally, but judiciously in appropriate instances to make sentences and paragraphs flow in proper order. These link words help information flow from one sentence to another. Some chronological linking words are: During, before, finally, in turn, earlier, previously, later, while, after, etc.

Examples of links showing cause and effect are: Therefore, since, because, based on, consequently, accordingly, etc.

Do this editing to make reading easy. Readers should not have to think too hard to read your book. Also look for word overuse. If you have used the word "beautiful" twice in the same sentence, substitute another word or change the sentence. Everyone has pet words and if they are popping up over and over, strike them. Overuse of is/are/was/were verbs will tempt you. I've seen histories and reports where every sentence reads, "She was born . . . She was the fourth child . . . She was a nice girl . . . She was a student at . . . She was married . . ." and so forth. Use other verbs or combine sentences. "A nice girl, she attended. . ." Rearrange sentences for variety. Make some short, others long. Don't start everyone of them the same way ("he did . . ." "he then did . . .")

"Copy editing" is correcting spelling, grammar, and fact checking. The rule on spelling is to use the dictionary more than you think you should! Grammar is trickier. Even the experts quibble over grammatical usage. Books and books will tell you the rules. But for our purposes, be sure you have the following usages down pat:

1) When you use three or more terms linked by a conjunction (such as "and") put a serial comma after each term except the last. *Clara, Samuel, and Benjamin*

2) Capitalize "Jr." and "Sr." and separate these distinctions from a proper name with a comma. *James Champion, Jr.*

3) Use semicolons (;) to separate commas. *Isabel Magruder, Long Beach, Calif.; Greg Boyer, Manhattan Beach, Calif.; and Vince Morgan, San Diego, Calif.*

4) Colons (:) are for lists. *Mark and Ann had five children: Molly, Sarah, James, Ellen, and Melissa*

Don't try to do all your editing steps at one time. It's exhaustive and you will miss errors. Nor should you look for all errors at the same time. Read for spelling errors, then again for consistency, etc. It doesn't take long to run through your manuscript to see if you have all state abbreviations after a city (*San Paulo, Calif.*) or spelled-out states (San Paolo, *California*). Then look for something else.

Finished? Put your work aside for a week. Then look at it again. It's amazing how many errors pop out. And in three months, there will be even more!

Chapter Seventeen

VISUAL ACCENTS

*I*llustrations are a great way to get and hold your reader's attention. Once you have your narrative (almost) written. think about your book's final appearance.

A popular size for printed books is 6" x 9", but printers can make any size with varying prices. We recommend 8 ½" x 11", because this size makes photograph placement easier and is the typical size of genealogical works. This format also works well for two-column pages, which, typically, read easier. If photocopying, you will probably use the 8 ½" x 11" format unless you fold the sheets in half to make 8 ½" x 5". This size can also be printed on 11" x 17" paper and folded with a saddle stitch (center staples) binding.

Paragraph Typography

Within each paragraph, you can assign information status visually. Many think that printing words in ALL CAPITAL LETTERS (e.g., headlines or chapter titles), gets attention. You do get attention, but at the sacrifice of legibility. Use this device sparingly, if at all. Putting reoccurring family surnames or introducing new family lines in all capitals is popular with some genealogists.

Italics highlight information in an unobtrusive manner. They are also good when you quote or lift several paragraphs directly from one source. Readability decreases a bit with italics, but less than that with the use of all capital letters.

Wrote Ehret: *The family first went to Clay Center, which had been . . .*

You get attention with boldface. On typewriters, you used to have to double strike on the letter for bolder print. Try not to overuse and make boldface splotches on every page, because the effect will lose its power. Also avoid underlining to draw attention. Underlining was a device used to signify importance when using typewriters and has been replaced by computer's boldface and italic print. Nevertheless, some people still cling to underlining and fancy it for headlines.

When typing with a computer, leave one space after an end punctuation mark. Spaces between paragraphs can give white space for reader relief.

PHOTOGRAPHS

If you have not already done so, contact all family members to gather photographs. When you borrow photographs, immediately make a note about the owner and his or her return address.

Temporarily attach photographs with rubber cement to your final manuscript when doing your final printing. When photocopying, use the photograph setting to eliminate high-contrast blacks and whites that obscure details. Photocopy only once, because subsequent photocopying darkens the image. So, if you want your photograph a different size, determine the correct reduction or enlargement on the first shot, then place that copy on your final manuscript.

Examine photographs before pasting and decide whether they need to be cropped. Cropping means to cut out the areas along photograph edges that detract from the image. If photocopying, cut the photocopy, not the photograph. Use scissors if you have to, but an X-Acto knife and metal ruler works best for cleaner edges. Print shops have cutting equipment you can also use. For publications to be professionally printed, tape photographs to a blank piece of paper and indicate on the paper the photograph edges to trim. Another way is to tape a piece of tissue paper over the photograph and mark cut lines on the tissue. You will also need to number photographs in the order they will appear in your book and indicate the final size (e.g., 100 percent means the same size; 75 percent means three-quarters the size, and so forth).

The best way for photograph reproduction is to have a print shop make halftones of the photographs.

The halftone process breaks the image into minute black dots that photocopy clearer and preserve gray tones. (Black and white photographs reproduce far better than color photographs.) A scanned photograph on a computer follows a similar process. When doing halftones, group several photographs together to save money. A book professionally printed will take care of this process for you. If you are doing it yourself at a photocopy store, you need to do this yourself before photocopying.

Each final illustration needs to be identified with a caption. In group shots, start with a certain row and identify people from left to right. In situations where the subjects are not in exact rows, list them starting at one side and add identifying notes.

From left: Alma Cyrs, Emmarie Simpson (wearing corsage), Violet Todd

Avoid numbering people on your photograph, then listing them underneath, because superimposed numbers detract from the photograph. If you have room, cite the source for the photograph in the caption.

Alma Cyrs and Violet Todd (Courtesy of Kevin Cyrs, Grand Island, Nebraska)

No room for including sources in the caption or at another place near the photograph? You could mention them in the text (e.g., the photograph of Alma Cyrs on this page was courtesy of Kevin Cyrs, Grand Island, Nebraska). To eliminate this distraction, a better method may be to cite photograph sources in a list in the back of the book. List photographs on certain pages that came from one source, the photographs that came from another, and so forth.

Photographs on pps. 13, 52, and 98, courtesy of Kevin Cyrs, Grand Island, Nebraska; pps. 17 and 18, courtesy of Heather Mater, . . .

Place captions under the illustration either to the right, left, or center—just be sure to place it consistently in the same spot.

BEYOND PHOTOGRAPHS

Source documents that you discovered during research can be very effective for visual accentuation. Certificates, military records, diary pages, school report cards, personal letters—reproduce them in full or use only a relevant portion. If they are hard to read, print the information and enlarge a small part of the original to give an idea of its appearance. If you are planning to add 50 pages of back-up documents to authenticate your findings, reconsider. That's a lot to muddle through. Put in your best ones and let your writing suffice.

Maps are almost a necessity for communicating information. Besides maps found in books and atlases, computers often have maps of each state or geographic sections. Office supply stores and bookstores also offer outline maps (blank maps) of the state, country, and world. To obtain more detailed maps, you can also contact the National Archives, Cartographic Archives Division, Washington, DC 20408, or the

Library of Congress, Geography and Map Division, James Madison Building, Washington, DC 20408 for maps of the early U.S. wards, county land ownership, county atlases from 1825 and other specific maps. National Archives also has Sanborn maps, which are insurance company maps dating from the mid-1800s. These detailed maps of densely populated cities show each town building complete with the number of stories, construction materials, use, etc.

Genealogical companies also offer maps, such as *Map Guide to Federal Census, 1790–1920* by William Thorndale and William Dollarhide (Genealogical Publishing, 1992) that offers hundreds of maps depicting county boundaries for each state. Many of these maps are on computer software programs (e.g., The Gold Bug, P. O. Box 588, Alamo, CA 94507, goldbug@aol.com with its 2,000 maps + on one program).

You may have to manipulate a map to custom fit information. That may mean enlarging a section of the map pertinent to your family, tracing an outline of a fuzzy reproduction to make your own map, or adding objects to the map. For instance, if your family has lived in many places, trace their migration by marking the area where they lived and indicate their migration with a straight line for one family, a dotted line for another, and so forth.

LINE ART

Wouldn't it be marvelous if you had a talented family member willing to illustrate your book and actually had the time to do it? The next best solution is to use "clip-art"—ready-made illustrations in the public domain that you can use for no fee or recognition. Graphically, these line-cut illustrations reduce and enlarge well because they are black and white without shades of gray. Some can be found in computer programs or in the Dover series of clip-art books offering historical depictions. A fertile source of line art can be found in older Sears and Montgomery Ward mail-order catalogs. Libraries often have these books in their reference sections. Town histories and old magazines are also a good source for line art.

CHARTS

When genealogists hear the word "charts," they think of pedigree, descendant, and drop-line charts showing ancestor relationships. Charts are a fun way to analyze and present information. Take your basic statistics—age of marriage, number of children, age at death—and you can have a field day making charts. Most word processing programs and genealogical programs have chart-making features.

ILLUSTRATION PLACEMENT

Where are you going to put the illustrations? Basically, you have two choices: You can lump illustrations in one section or throughout the text. Most prefer to put the illustration by the text reference—you'll want to leave the area blank and paste in the illustration before it is time to publish—but that can get tricky if you make subsequent text changes. Use rubber cement to paste illustrations, because it makes for easy removal. Be sure to clean up any rubber cement around the sides. Spray adhesive also works well. All edges need to be firmly adhered to prevent dark lines appearing in the final copy.

The world of computers changes daily. At this time, you may use a computer scanner rather than photocopying. Make sure the resolution is sufficient; if not, place illustrations manually.

Chapter Eighteen

PACKAGING THE STORY

CONTENTS

Once your narrative is complete, spend time on finishing touches. First off, end your story. Wrapping up with a summary is a time-honored ending style. Your sentiments about the significance of the family history are also relevant. Another ingredient to consider is an outside quotation, such as: Carl Sandburg wrote, "When a society or a civilization perishes, one condition can always be found. They forgot where they came from." Add a piece of advice (e.g., "Live in peace.") and you will have a strong ending.

Your narrative history does not stand alone. It is preceded by "front matter," namely:

Publication Title

Title Page
Table of Contents

Other pages that may comprise this front matter are:

Foreword
Introduction or About the Author/About the
Book
Acknowledgments
Dedication

and because this is a family history, consider including:

Time Chart
Numbering Explanation
Family Name Definition
Family Coat of Arms
Family Characteristics Page
Abbreviations Used

FRONTMATTER

TITLE

You might have decided your title before you wrote your book. Or the title might have occurred to you while writing. But, if you are like most of us, picking a title takes thought. You could use simply the names of the family founders, then add the dates, and list related families, such as:

James Paine and Mary Bailey: 1880–2002,
Related Families include Bonebrake, Groninger,
Hibbs, Kelley, and others.

(In your history you might have related surnames. While you could list all in the subtitle, it might be more appropriate to list only the surnames of direct antecedents, and, in some cases, surnames of those for whom you have extensive information.) When you decide on your title, put it on a separate page for your cover, centered two to four inches down from the top margin.

TITLE PAGE

This is the first written page of your book. It includes your title, name, publication date, and sometimes your address (which helps for future orders or correspondence). It does not have a page number. Center the title about one-third down the page.

COPYRIGHT PAGE

Copyright means that only an author has the right to reproduce (e.g., photocopy), distribute copies, or prepare derivative works (such as a movie) from the work. Copyright laws currently protect your work from being reprinted by another for your lifetime + 50 years. It does not protect the information in your book; if someone wants to paraphrase your information and issue their own book, that is legal. To make the copyright symbol, write the word "Copyright", place a C in a circle beside the year published, and then write your name: Copyright ©2000 by Jane Jones.

If you are including a copyright page, place it right behind the title page. Other information on this page would include publisher name, date, any previous printings, a Library of Congress Cataloging number (or other cataloging numbers, e.g., ISBN). Contact the Library of Congress at Washington, DC 20559-6000, or call 202-707-3000. You will fill out an application form and send the Library two books.

Table of Contents

List chapter titles and page numbers on this right-hand page. If you are including foreword (see next listing), place the word "Foreword" before chapter titles. You may want, if you have room, to list illustrations on this page. Illustrations may also be listed with their page numbers on the following page (entitled "List of Illustrations" or other applicable phrase). If these illustrations are on pages without numbers, you can denote them with "following page 15" and other place indicators.

Foreword

The foreword is an introduction written by somebody other than the author. This probably is not needed in most family history cases, but is necessary in some. Traditionally, a foreword and following introduction are numbered with Roman numerals separately from the text numbering. They begin on the right-hand side of a book.

Preface

A preface is written by the author to briefly describe how and why the book was written. You might divide the preface into an *About the Author* page followed by an *About the Book* page containing your summary. Often authors request that readers suggest corrections for when they revise the publication. At the end of your preface, it is a nice touch to sign your name.

INTRODUCTION

If your introduction is part of your narrative, number its pages as the start of the book's first chapter. Introductions are a good place to discuss the family homeland before emigration.

ACKNOWLEDGMENTS

This right-hand page (the back is left blank) is where you express thanks to all those who helped you research and prepare the book. You might have pages of people to thank or only one. Sources used can also be mentioned in this section. Put acknowledgments on a separate page, or place acknowledgments on the same page as contents, introduction, etc.

DEDICATION

Always on the book right hand side, this page is where you express appreciation succinctly and its back is left blank. Since it is a family history, you might want to dedicate the work to your favorite relative. Then again, you don't have to dedicate your book to a person. Dedicate it to an abstract quality ("perseverance"), an animal ("Scrapper, my terrier, who sat by my side through many revisions") or other motivator. This could also be a nice location for a quotation about family history. Here are a few examples:

With him for a sire and her for a dam, What should I be but just what I am?—Edna St. Vincent Millay

To forget one's ancestors is to be a brook without a source, a tree without a root.—Chinese proverb

The past sharpens perspective, warns of pitfalls, and helps to point the way.—Dwight D. Eisenhower

Memory is where the proof of life is stored. It offers material for stock-taking and provides clues about where our lives are going.—Norman Cousins

TIME CHARTS

Time charts can list relevant family events, which could lead to a host of things or only marriage dates. To make them easier to grasp, incorporate outside historical events on your chart.

FAMILY CHARACTERISTICS PAGE

This page works well preceding or following your narrative. Think about it. Isn't your mother's side of the family different from your father's side? Of course it is. Every family has unique traits that stamp, to a certain degree, the individuals in it. Delve into your families' social activities, religious practices, education, political attitude, and military service—are you seeing any similarities? Is your extended family conservative? Adventurous? Ambitious? What is the nature of family courtships—

quick, formal, arranged? Does your family have any "stars?" Black sheep? Is there a common physical appearance or reoccurring physical characteristic? ("Rita Kraus says a crooked toe next to the smallest toe runs in the Kraus family. Several members have had this toe that slides under the one next to it.") Does your family suffer any chronic illnesses or deformities? How did generations of your family earn a living? If you include this page in your completed history, it will be the one readers are sure to remember!

BACKMATTER

APPENDICES

The appendices are where anything goes—supporting documents, life span charts, maps, short family histories written by others, lengthy letters too distracting for the main text, examples . . . anything you find of interest or added illumination. Different materials would be treated as separate chapters and titled Appendix A, Appendix B, and so forth.

RELATED FAMILIES

While doing your research, you probably found some suspected relatives. Often, writers wait to the end before including a section on relatives whom they highly believe are related, but lack hard proof. Keeping them to the end keeps the main section historically accurate. Then again, in telling your tale and trying to guide your relative through it with minimal confusion, you might have skimmed over or eliminated extended family members. Or you have scads more information on one family in particular. To balance your work, you might include these overflows in a special appendix, perhaps "Indirect Relations" or "More on the Hughes Family."

GLOSSARY

If you are using terms unfamiliar to your readers, a glossary provides them with simple explanations. This is also helpful if you are using words or phrases in a different language.

CURRENT FAMILY ADDRESSES

Having contact information for relatives makes it convenient for all to contact each other. Unfortunately, addresses change so often that your information may be out of date almost as soon as you write it! Nevertheless, it is a starting point for family exchange.

FAMILY HEIRLOOMS

Every family has items with special meaning. These special things may be expensive, hand made, noteworthy because of their owner, or special because of other reasons. A listing of these items might be something you would want to add to your publication. Here's an example from one family that included photographs of each heirloom:

Secretary desk: Piece said to be brought from Wales by Tippers and had been handed down to the oldest son for generations. The upper section with curved cut-out wood ornamentation has glassed-in shelves. It sits on the desk section with an enclosed space below. During its last move, the desk flap was damaged and replaced. In possession of William Sanders at Lane, Kansas.

Bible: Dating to 1886, this large Bible contains births, deaths, and marriages of various family members. Later dates were entered by Sabrina Short and Sienna Blair. In possession of James Short, Moore, OK.

Christening gown. From Robert Blair family. Now in possession of Susan Short, Oklahoma City, Oklahoma.

FAMILY DATA SHEETS

These records were the source for your narrative. If you need to recopy them in a more legible format, do so. If you make your own, you can leave space to write in findings after the book is published. If you are using computer print-outs and can number them on the computer, that is great. Otherwise, hand number or paste on numbers, so that these sheets can be found easily. You can alphabetize each family group, but place them in order of the earliest ancestor and work forward in time. You may find it easier to alphabetize each individual or other method.

INDEX

Have you ever picked up a book and realized you had to read the entire book to see if your relative was in there?

That's why you need an index. Librarians especially find indexes helpful when they assist patrons. To do a surname index, list each name as it appears in your book and the pages where the name is found.

Rose, John (1801–1837), 10, 12
Nellie (1820–1821) 12
William (1849–1937) 55, 63
Suelle, Mary (1898–1963) 89-93

A first name index can be useful if the majority of relatives have the same name.

In your index, list people with variant name spellings . . .

Smith, Mary, p. 57
Smythe, Mary (see Mary Smith)

. . . and multiple marriages, too.

Hill, Cecille
Murdock, Cecille (Pyeatt) (Hill)
Pyeatt, Cecille (Hill)

If you want to make your index smaller, after your final typing is done, reduce the pages by photocopy. Then paste-up the reduced text on new pages. Be sure to note if you are indexing all names or only those names in your main narrative.

AFTERWORD

In this last update, sometimes known as an "Addendum" when new information is added or an

"Errata" when corrections to the printed text are made, you get your last chance to write. Some people use this section to ask readers for information for a new edition or for an expanded version of the original.

CAMERA READY?

Your final print of front matter, narrative, and back matter should be on good quality paper and be run from a laser printer. To attach illustrations, you will need supplies, including an adhesive (removable tape, rubber cement, glue stick, art glue spray), white correction fluid, a sharp tip knife, scissors, ruler, and a t-square if you have one to make sure illustrations line-up horizontally and vertically. When done, go through your pages one more time. Look for any smudges, stray lines, glue bits, etc. If you have pages that do not have printed numbers, indicate page numbers to yourself or the printer by using a special non-reproducible blue pencil available at art or print shops.

PRINTER TYPES AND ESTIMATES

Professional printers do a large-volume trade and do not do small print runs (less than 500 books). Or if they do, the cost will be high. You may want to contact a printer advertising in genealogical literature, because that printer is specialized in the publishing you want. Offset-printing shops may also be able to print your publication from your computer disk.

These first two options take a film negative of each page, and paste together the negatives in a signature to make a plate that is then mounted on a printing press. These plates may be made of metal, paper, or other materials. Usually, a picture ("blueline") is made of this plate and given to you to ensure your satisfaction. The more copies you make, the less each individual copy will be.

The local photocopying store, of course, can print you as few or as many copies as you want. Before you make a decision, shop around. Contact at least three printers. Be prepared to tell printers your publication.

Figure 8: PRINTING TERMS

Bleed: Printed images that extend beyond the page

Camera-ready art: Exact material that is to be printed with no alterations required

Copy: Furnished material (manuscript, art, etc) to be used in printing production

Crop: Indicated portions of the image not to be used

Dummy: Layout showing position of art and text as they will appear in final printed piece

Halftone: A print that converts an image into dots of various sizes

Line art: Solid black and white copy without any gray colors

PMS: Method of identifying a particular ink color with a number

Paste-up: Positioning of type and line are as it will appear in final form

Transparency: Photographic film viewed by light (i.e., 35 mm slide)

details (e.g., 8 ½" x 11" size, 20 lb. bond paper, soft cover, 31 photographs, 180 pages, and 32 final copies).

PAPER

Final pages for copying should be on white, medium weight paper for clarity. Black ink on white paper offers the best contrast. Stay away from onion skin papers; they are not durable and are too transparent. Paper comes in weights. Typing paper is general 20# bond (the # means pound), which is less opaque than heavier papers. Don't get paper heavier than 60 pounds, because you are only adding weight and cost to your final project with no rewards. Use white paper, and be forewarned that the whiteness will diminish in time, especially if exposed to sunlight or ultraviolet light. Steer away from slick, enamel-coated papers—they are not long-lived.

Your paper should contain little or no acid because acid deteriorates. Before photocopying, do a test print first and see how well the ink stays on.

PAGE PLACEMENT

Decide now whether you are going to have print on one side of your pages or if you are using both front and back of each sheet. If you plan on using front and back, you may want to insert blank sheets after certain pages that should have a blank back. For instance, title sheets, table of contents, dedications, section changes, and the appendix generally lies on the right side of a book. (Confusing? Tell the printer or photocopy shop the order of pages you want.)

Those who are getting their book professionally printed should be aware that printers determine the number of pages by a signature—a large piece of paper folded, then cut—not the actual number of pages you give them. Generally, this means that you can have a total number of pages divisible by four.

BINDING

You can bind your work at home by punching holes in your sheets and binding them in a 3-ring notebook or with brads. While not elegant, it does make for easy page replacement and updating. Photocopy stores offer tape binding, channel (or perfect) binding, plastic or wire spiral bound (1.5 inch or less thick), and hard cover binding. Cover pages can be printed on ordinary paper, cardstock, clear acetate, or vinyl (our current favorite). If you want your book to be hardbound and have gold lettering on the front, but don't want many copies, consider having it bound similar to college theses and dissertations. This will give your book a sturdy covering with text for about $15 a copy. The work must by 8 ½" x 11" and no thicker than two inches (400 pages.) Look for this binding under "Thesis service" in the yellow pages of your telephone book. If your work is going to a printer, it can either be:

- Saddle-Stitch: Economical, for books up to 64 pages, this type of binding with wire stitched through the fold allows the book to lay flat when open

- Side-Stitched/Side-stapled: Single sheets are stitched at the side and overlaid with tape binding. This type of binding does not allow the book to lay flat.

- Perfect binding: This is what you see at bookstores, where papers are glued on the side and a paper cover is glued on top. It does not have long life span.

- Edition binding: Thread is inserted in folds every 32 pages, with each section glued in between a hard cover.

- Library binding: This is the strongest of all bindings, with single sheets sewn together before the entire book is glued with a hard cover.

COVER

A simple, effective way to make your cover look nice is to center your information on the page, use a border, and a simple illustration. The type of cover stock paper or material (e.g., vinyl) you use will also influence its final appearance. Be wary of using ink-jet colors on the cover, because they fade.

HOW MANY TO PRINT?

How many do you plan to print? One way to get a good estimate is to round up buyers before you print.

Tell potential buyers that the book is available and ask for advance orders.

Dear PERSON,

After many years of work, I have finally compiled TITLE. This work begins with PERSON/DATE and ends DATE. Allied families include: FAMILY SURNAMES LIST. The printed work at this time is projected to be SIZE, PAGE LENGTH, and COST. Order now for Christmas, birthdays, anniversaries, and future generations. Please tell me by DATE how many you are interested in buying.

Sincerely,

YOUR NAME

Do this by postcard or letter. Include an order form for best results. Set a deadline for responses. Don't get downhearted if many do not respond. Once they hear about or see the printed copy, you will have more requests for copies.

Another pre-sell method is to put a notice in genealogical publications (*see Figure 9*). With thousands of genealogical publications (newspaper columns, newsletters, magazines, etc.) in circulation, you have several from which to chose. Look at your library for reference books and periodicals that list current genealogical offerings. When submitting your notice, make it short or send a flyer.

PRESERVING FAMILY HISTORIES

First, place a copy with other valuable family records. Local and state historical societies are interest-

Figure 9: SAMPLE NOTICE

The Riley Chronicles: 1794-2001
The Riley family, one of southwest Arizona's first pioneer families, has finally received the attention it deserves!

The Riley Chronicles, by Aaron McMalone, is the first full-length treatment of this adventuring Irish family. From Ulster to the Carolinas and along the western trails, this family chronicle spans three centuries in a highly readable style.

The 173-page, hard cover book includes rare documents, photographs, maps, and numerous other illustrations as well as a 1,750-name index. Allied families include: Hiatt, Athas, Green, Donohues, Bailey, and Heller.

Order now. $20 prepaid.
History Press
737 Medina Way
Bakersfield, OH 65332

ed in family histories, as are, quite often, local colleges and universities. If you think no one would be interested in your history, you are wrong. A family history is a valuable resource for researchers of the American past and family members to come.

If you wish to safeguard the privacy of family members, write in the history that you wish no names of living persons obtained from the history to be used without your permission. When depositing your work, attach a manuscript describing the terms of your donation and the rights of the institution receiving it.

ᴊ might want to register your book with the
ʀy of Congress, which lets libraries through the
world know what books it has available. To apply,
write for forms to:

Publications Section, LM-455
Copyright Office
Library of Congress
Washington, DC 20559-6000
202-707-9100

There will be a minimal cost for a number and listing,
and you will have send them a final manuscript.
Periodicals will review your book in exchange for com-
plimentary copy. Try Everton Publishers in Logan,
Utah, and remember to include the price of your book
and where it can be purchased. This is a good way to
sell copies if your family is large or if you have several
families listed. You can also receive order forms from
libraries and historical societies. Send notices to public
libraries, research centers, university libraries, etc.

Chapter Nineteen

SHARING YOUR FAMILY HISTORY

CELEBRATE YOUR SUCCESS WITH A FAMILY REUNION

*B*ringing together your extended family is a marvelous goal to strive for when researching your family roots. In today's hectic age, a family heritage is more important than ever.

The best way to go about arranging your family reunion is to plan ahead and ask family members to help! Scout locations (one significant to the family, ideally), create a mailing list, and set a date (three-day weekends are good). Next, if you want, choose a theme that you can incorporate into communications and events. When planning food, don't feel as if you have to stick with the traditional potlucks or barbecues.

You can plan a menu around the food associated with your homeland, go to a restaurant, or have everything catered.

REUNION ACTIVITIES

Plan both outside and inside activities, but have back-up plans in case of bad weather.

What to do? You can have contests, such as water balloon tossing, indoor Olympics, volleyball, or more sedentary pursuits (e.g., chess and guessing games). Stage an honors ceremony and single out family members for graduations, promotions, retirement, marriages, new babies, and other traditional milestones. It doesn't have to be too serious. You also can give out awards for best bubble gum chewing, strangest color for a car, and other made-up categories. Or make a cookbook of recipes and sell it at the reunion!

Assign skits, especially ones based on the family history. Ask families to make up their own cheers and let them share their creations at a family sing-along by the campfire. Host a movie night with popcorn and ask everyone to bring a video tape of an event from the last year.

If your family members are good at crafts and art, ask them to bring a sample for display. You might even want to hold an auction and donate proceeds to a charity.

COUNTDOWN TO THE REUNION

Reserve a block of rooms at a nearby hotel and send out a mailer with the tentative reunion schedule and cost. Include names of missing relatives, so that others may be able to help you find their locations. A month or two in advance, reserve rental equipment (e.g., tables, chairs, microphone, etc.) and confirm sleeping and eating accommodations. If you are going to have a photographer, book as early as you can.

The day before the reunion, set up registration tables, rental equipment, and displays. Decorate with a table of vintage photos and have your relatives guess which family members are in the photographs. You may want to post a giant family tree so all can see where they fit in the family.

If you think some may be uncomfortable at first, work some "ice breakers" into the initial activities. For instance, you can ask everyone to stand in circle and have each person say his or her name before pantomiming a favorite hobby. Once the hobby is guessed, it is the next person's turn.

Another ice breaker is to have everyone together, then tell them to form groups by what distinction— "everyone with curly hair, or everyone who likes to fish or everyone who knows how to polka"—is called out.

BE PREPARED

Have plenty of copies of the material you have collected during your search available for everyone to see, including family group charts, photographs, newspaper clippings, certificates, and the like. Also, have copies of your printed family history on hand. You will probably hear more stories and new facts, so keep those in mind for your revised family history edition! If you haven't finished your final family history, then take advantage of the reunion to take photographs and notes!

Appendix

STATE REPOSITORIES

Alabama
Alabama Archives & History
Department
P. O. Box 300100
Montgomery, AL 36130-0100
334-242-4435

Alaska
Alaska Historical Library
Juneau, AK 99801

Alaska State Library
http://www.educ.state.ak.us/lam/
library.html

Arizona
Arizona State Library
Archives & Public Records
1700 W. Washington
State Capitol
Phoenix, AZ 85007
http://www.dlapr.lib.az.us/

Arkansas
Arkansas State Library
One Capitol Mall
Little Rock, Arkansas 72201
501-682-2053
http://www.asl.lib.ar.us/

California
California State Library
P. O. Box 942837
914 Capitol Mall
Sacramento, CA 94237-0001
http://www.library.ca.gov/

Colorado
Stephen A. Hart Library
Colorado Historical Society
1300 Broadway
Denver, CO 80203
303-866-2305
http://www.gtownloop.com/chs.html

Connecticut
Connecticut State Library
History and Genealogy Unit
231 Capitol Avenue
Hartford, CT 06106-1537
http://www.cslnet.ctstateu/edu/

Delaware

Delaware Public Archives
Hall of Records
Dover, DE 19901
302-739-5318
http://del-aware.lib.de.us/archives

Delaware Division of
Libraries
http://www.lib.de.us/

District of Columbia

District of Columbia Public
Library
901 G Street NW
Washington, DC 20001
202-727-0321
http://dclibrary.org/

Florida

Florida State Library
http://stafla.dlis.state.fl.us/

Indian River County Main
Library
Florida History and
Genealogy Department
1600 21st Street
Vero Beach, FL 32960
561-770-5060

Georgia

Georgia Public Library
Services
1800 Century Place
Atlanta, GA 30345
404-982-3560

Georgia Department of
Archives and History
330 Capitol Avenue SE
Atlanta, GA 30334
404-656-2393
http://www.sos.state.ga.us/archives

Georgia Historical Society
Library
501 Whittaker Street
Savannah, GA 31401
http://www.savannah-online.com/ghs/

Hawaii

Library of Hawaii
King & Punchbowl Sts.
Honolulu, HI 96813

Idaho

Idaho Genealogical Library
325 W. State
Boise, ID 83702

Idaho State Historical Society
Library
450 N. 4th Street
Boise, ID 83702
208-334-3357

University of Idaho Library
Special Collections
Moscow, ID 83844-2351
208-885-7951
http://www.lib.uidaho.edu/
special-collections/

Illinois

Illinois State Archives
Archives Building
Springfield, IL 62756

Illinois State Historical
Library
Old State Capitol
Springfield, IL 62706
http://www.state.il.us/hpa/lib/

Illinois State Library
300 S. Second Street
Springfield, IL 62701-1796
217-785-5600
http://www.sos.state.il.us/depts/library/
isl_home.html

Indiana

Indiana Historical Society
Library
315 W. Ohio Street
Indianapolis, IN 46202-3299
317-232-1879
http://www.dghd.com/ihs1830/
manarch.htm

Indiana State Library
Genealogy Division
140 N. Senate Avenue
Indianapolis, IN 46204
317-232-3689
http://www.statelib.lib.in.us/

Iowa

State Library of Iowa
1112 East Grand
Des Moines, IA 50319
512-281-4105
http://www.silo.lib.ia.us/

State Historical Society of
Iowa
600 E. Locust
Des Moines, IA 50319
http://www.state.ia.us/government/dca

Kansas

Kansas State Historical
Society
6425 SW Sixth Avenue
Topeka, KS 66615
785-272-8681
http://www.kshs.org

Kansas Library
300 S. W. 10th Avenue
Topeka, KS 66612-1593
785-296-3296
http://skyways.lib.ks.us/kansas/KSL/

Kentucky

Kentucky Department for
Libraries and Archives
P. O. Box 537
300 Coffee Tree Rd.
Frankfort, KY 40602-0537
502-564-8794
http://www.kdla.state.ky.us/

Louisiana

New Orleans Public Library
219 Loyola Avenue
New Orleans, LA 70112-2049
504-596-2610
http://www.gnofn.org/~nopl/guides/
genguide/ggcover.htm

State Library of Louisiana
P. O. Box 31
701 N. 4th Street
Baton Rouge, LA 70821-0131
504-342-4914
http://smt.state.lib.la.us/

Maine

Maine State Library
http://www.state.me.us/msl/

Maryland

Enoch Pratt Library
400 Cathedral Street
Baltimore, MD 21201-4484
410-396-5468
http://www.pratt.lib.md.us/pratt/
depts/md

Maryland State Archives
350 Rowe Boulevard
Annapolis, MD 21401
410-974-3914
http://www.mdarchives.state.md.us/

Maryland State Library
361 Rose Boulevard
Annapolis, MD 21401

Massachusetts
State Library of
Massachusetts
341 State House
Boston, MA 02133
617-727-2590
http://www.mlin.lib.ma.us

Massachusetts State Archives
220 Morrissey Boulevard
Boston, MA 02125
617-727-2816
http://www.magnet.state.ma.us/sec/
arc/arcfam/famidx.htm

Michigan
Michigan Library
717 West Allegan
P. O. Box 30007
Lansing, MI 48909-7507
http://www.libofmich.lib.mi.us/

State Archives of Michigan
Michigan Historical Center
717 W. Allegan Street
Lansing, MI 48918-1837
517-373-1408
http://www.sos.state.mi.us/history/
archive/archive.html

Minnesota
Minnesota Historical Society
345 Kellog Boulevard West
Street Paul, MN 55102-1906
651-296-6126
http://www.mnhs.org/ebranch/mhs/
index.html

Mississippi
Mississippi Library Commission
1221 Ellis Ave.
Jackson, MS 39289
601-961-4111
http://www.mlc.lib.ms.us:80/

Missouri
Mid-Continent Public Library
Genealogy Department
317 W. 24 Hiway
Independence, MO
816-252-0950
http://www.mcpl.lib.mo.us

Missouri State Archives
600 W. Main Street
P. O Box 778
Jefferson City, MO 65102

Kansas City Public Library
Heart of America
Genealogical Society
311 E. 12th Street
Kansas City, MO 64106-2412

Montana
Montana State Library
http://msl.mt.gov/

Nebraska
Nebraska Library
Commission
http:/www.nlc.state.ne.us

Nebraska State Historical
Society Library
1500 R Street
Lincoln, NE 68508
402-471-4751

Nevada
Nevada State Library and
Archives
http://www.clan.lib.nv.us/docs/
NSLA/nsla.htm

Nevada State Historical
Society Library
P. O. Box 1192
Reno, NV 89501

New Hampshire
New Hampshire State
Library
20 Park Street
Concord, NH 03301
603-271-6823
http://www.state.nh.us/nhsl

New Jersey
New Jersey State Library
185 W. State Street
Trenton, NJ 08625-0520
609-292-6274
http://www.njstatelib.org

New Mexico
Albuquerque Public Library
423 East Central Avenue NE
Albuquerque, NM 87101

New Mexico State Library
http://www.stlib.state.nm.us/

New York
New York Public Library
Fifth Avenue and 42nd Street
New York, NY 10018
212-930-0828
http://www.nypl.org

New York State Archives
Cultural Education Center
Albany, NY 12230
518-474-8955
http://www.sara.nysed.gov/

North Carolina
North Carolina Archives and
Reports
109 E. Jones Street
Raleigh, NC 27611
http://www.ah.dcr.state.nc.us/

State Library of North
Carolina
http://statelibrary.dcr.state.nc.us/

North Dakota
North Dakota State Library
604 E. Boulevard Avenue
Bismarck, ND 58506
http://ndsl.lib.state.nd.us/

Ohio
Ohio Historical Society
Library
1985 Velma Avenue
Columbus, OH 43211

Libraries in Ohio
http://www.acclaimed.com/help-ful/oh-lib.htm

Oklahoma
Oklahoma Department of
Libraries
http://www.state.ok.us/~odl

Oklahoma Historical Society
Library
2100 N. Lincoln Avenue
Oklahoma City, OK 73105
405-522-5225
http://www.ohiohistory.org

Oregon
Oregon Genealogical
Society Library
223 North A Street
Suite F
Springfield, OR 97477
541-746-7924
http://www.rootsweb.com/orlncogs/

Oregon Historical Society
Library
1230 SW Park Avenue
Portland, OR 97201

Oregon State Archives
1005 Broadway NE
Salem, OR 97301
503-373-0701
http://arcweb.sos.state.or.us/

Pennsylvania
Historical Society of
Pennsylvania Library
1300 Locust Street
Philadelphia, PA 19107-5699
215-732-6200
http://www.libertynet.org/~pahist

Pennsylvania State Library
P. O. Box 1601
Harrisburg, PA 17105-1601
717-787-4440

Rhode Island

Providence Public Library
225 Washington Street
Providence, RI 02903
401-455-8000
http://www.clan.lib.ri.us/provide.htm

Rhode Island Historical
Society Library
121 Hope Street
Providence, RI 02903

Rhode Island State Archives
314 State House
Providence, RI 02900

South Carolina

South Carolina State Library
1500 Senate Street
Columbia, SC 29211
803-734-8666
http://www.state.sc.us/scsl/

South Carolina Archives and
History
P. O. Box 11669
Columbia, SC 29211
803-734-8577
http://www.scdah.sc.edu/homepage.
htm

South Dakota

South Dakota State Library
800 Governor's Drive
Pierre, SC 57501
605-773-3131
http://www.state.sd.us/state/executive/
deca/st_lib/st_lib.htm

South Dakota State Archives
900 Governor's Drive
Pierre, SD 57501
605-773-3804
http://www.state.sd.us/state/executive/
deca/cultural/archives.htm

Tennessee

Tennessee State Library and
Archives
403 7th Avenue N
Nashville, TN 37203
615-741-2764
http://www.state.tn.us/sos/statelib/
tslahome.htm

Texas

Texas State Library and
Archives
1201 Brazos Street
Box 12917
Austin, TX 78711-2917
512-463-5463
http://www.tsl.state.tx.us/lobby

Utah

Utah State Historical Society
Library
300 Rio Grande
Salt Lake City, UT 84101

Utah State Archives
P. O. Box 141021
Salt Lake City, UT
84114-1021
801-538-3012
http://www.archives.state.ut.us/

Vermont

Vermont Department of
Libraries
109 State Street
Montpelier, VT 05609-0601
802-828-3261
http://dol.state.vt.us

Virginia

Library of Virginia
800 East Broad Street
Richmond, VA 23219
804-692-3500
http://www.lva.lib.va.us

Virginia Historical Society
Library
P. O. Box 7311
428 North Boulevard
Richmond, VA 23221
804-358-4901
http://www.vahistorical.org

Washington

Washington Public Libraries
Online
http://www.statelib.wa.gov/walo

West Virginia

West Virginia History
Collection
Colson Hall
West Virginia University
Library
Morgantown, WV 26506-6464
304-293-3536

Wisconsin

Wisconsin Historical Society
Library
816 State Street
Madison, WI 53706
608-264-6460

Wyoming

Laramie County Public Library
Genealogy Department
2800 Central Avenue
Cheyenne, WY 82001
307-634-3561

Wyoming State Archives and
Historical Department
2301 Central Avenue
Cheyenne, WY 82001
http://commerce.state.wy.us/CR/Archives

VITAL RECORDS

Alabama

Center for Health Statistics
State Department of Public
Health
P. O. Box 5625
434 Monroe Street
Montgomery, AL 36130
334-206-5418
Marriage: 1936–
Birth and death: 1908–
Divorce: 1950–

Alaska

Department of Health
Sciences and Social Services
Bureau of Vital Statistics
P. O. Box 110675
Juneau, AK 99811
907-465-3391
Marriage, birth, and death: 1913–

Arizona

Vital Records Section
Arizona Department of Health
Services
P. O. Box 3887
Phoenix, AZ 85030
602-255-3260
Marriage and divorce: Write county
Birth and death: 1909–

Arkansas

Division of Vital Records
Arkansas Department of Health
4815 West Markham Street
Little Rock, AR 72201
501-661-2336
Marriage: 1917–
Birth and death: 1914–
Divorce: 1923–

California

Vital Statistics Section
Department of Health Services
410 N. Street
P. O. Box 730241
Sacramento, CA 94244
916-445-2684
Marriage, birth, and death: 1905–

Colorado

Vital Records Section
Colorado Department of Health
4300 Cherry Creek Drive South
Denver, CO 80246
303-756-4454
http://www.cdphe.state.co.us/hs/
cshom.html
Marriage and death: 1900–
Birth: 1910

Connecticut
Vital Records
Department of Health
Services
410 Capitol Ave.
Hartford, CT 06134
203-566-1124
*Send request to town where event
occurred.*

Delaware
Office of Vital Statistics
Division of Public Health
P. O. Box 637
Dover, DE 19903
302-739-4721
Marriage: 1958–
Birth: 1926–
Death: 1958–

For earlier years, contact:
Archives Hall of Records
Dover, DE
302-739-5318

District of Columbia
Vital Records Branch
800 9th Street, SW.
Washington, DC 20024
202-645-5962
Birth: 1874–
Death: 1855–

For marriages, contact:
Marriage Bureau
515 5th Street, NW
Washington, DC 20001

Florida
Department of Health
Office of Vital Statistics
1217 Pearl Street
P. O. Box 210
Jacksonville, FL 32231
904-359-6900
Marriage: 1927–
Birth: 1865–
Death: 1877–
*The majority of birth and death
records date from 1917.*

Georgia
Department of Human
Resources
Vital Records Unit
Room 217-H
47 Trinity Avenue SW
Atlanta, GA 30334
404-656-4900
Marriage and divorce: 1952–
*(Requests for earlier dates will be
forwarded to appropriate county)*
Birth and death: 1919–

Hawaii

Office of Health Status
State Department of Health
P. O. Box 3378
Honolulu, HI 96801
808-586-4533
http://www.hawaii.gov/health/
sdohpg02.htm
Marriage, birth, and death: 1853–
Divorce: 1951–

Idaho

Vital Statistics Unit
Department of Health and
Welfare
450 West State Street
Boise, ID 83720
208-334-5988
Marriage and divorce: 1947–
Birth and death: 1911–

Illinois

Division of Vital Records
Department of Public Health
605 West Jefferson Street
Springfield, IL 62702
217-782-6553
Marriage and divorce: 1962–
Birth and death: 1916–

Indiana

Vital Records Section
State Department of Health
2 North Median Street
Indianapolis, IN 46204
317-233-2700
http://www.state.in.us/doh/index.html
Marriage: 1958–
Birth and death: 1907–

Iowa

Department of Public Health
Vital Records Section
Lucas Office Building
321 East 12th Street
Des Moines, IA 50319
515-281-4944
http://www.idph.state.ia.us/pa/vr.htm
Marriage, birth, and death: 1880–

Kansas

Office of Vital Statistics
State Department of Health
and Environment
900 Jackson Street, SW
Topeka, KS 66612
785-296-1400
Marriage: 1913–
Birth and death: 1911–

Kentucky

Office of Vital Statistics
Department for Health
Services
275 East Main Street
Frankfort, KY 40621
502-564-4212
Marriage: 1958–
Birth and death: 1911–

Louisiana

Vital Records Registry
Office of Public Health
325 Loyola Avenue
New Orleans, LA 70112
504-568-5152
Marriage: Contact parish
Birth and death: 1914–

City of New Orleans only
Bureau of Vital Statistics
City of Health Department
City Hall
Civic Center
New Orleans, LA 70112
Birth: 1892–
Death: 1942–

Older records for Louisiana
can be found at:
Louisiana State Archives
P. O. Box 94125
Baton Rouge, LA 70804

Maine

Office of Vital Records
Human Services Building
Station 11
State House
Augusta, ME 04333
207-287-3181
Marriage, birth, and death: 1892–

Maryland

Division of Vital Records
Department of Health and
Mental Hygiene
P. O. Box 68760
Baltimore, MD 21215
410-764-3038
Marriage: 1951–
Birth and death: 1898–

See also:
State of Maryland Archives
350 Rowe Blvd.
Annapolis, MD 21401
410-974-3914

City of Baltimore only
Bureau of Vital Statistics
Municipal Office Building
Baltimore, MD 21202
Birth and death: 1875–

Massachusetts

Registry of Vital Records and
Statistics
470 Atlantic Avenue
Boston, MA 02110
617-753-8600
Marriage, birth, and death: 1906–

For earlier recods, contact:
The Massachusetts Archives
at Columbia Point
220 Morrissey Boulevard
Boston, MA 02125
617-727-2816

Michigan

Office of the State Registrar
Department of Public Health
3423 North Martin Luther
King Boulevard
Lansing, MI 48909
517-335-8656
http://www.mdch.state.mi.us/pha/osr
Marriage, birth, and death: 1867–

Minnesota

Department of Health
Section of Vital Statistics
717 Delaware Street SE
P. O. Box 9441
Minneapolis, MN 55440
612-676-5120
http://www.health.state.mn.us
Marriage: 1958–
Birth: 1900–
Death: 1908–

Mississippi

Vital Records
State Department of Health
2423 North State Street
Jackson, MS 39216
601-576-7981
Marriage: 1926–1938; 1942–
Birth and death: 1912–

Missouri

Department of Health
Bureau of Vital Records
P. O. Box 570
Jefferson City, MO 65102
573-751-6400
http://www.health.state.mo.us/
cgibin/uncgi/BirthandDeathRecords
Marriage: 1948–
Birth and death: 1910–

Montana
Vital Statistics Bureau
Public Health and Human Services
1400 Broadway
P. O. Box4210
Helena, MT 59604
406-444-4228
http://www.dphhs.mt.gov
Marriage: 1943–
Birth and death: 1907–

Nebraska
Bureau of Vital Statistics
State Department of Health
301 Centennial Mall South
P. O. Box 95065
Lincoln, NE 68509
402-471-2871
Marriage: 1909–
Birth and death: 1904–

Nevada
Division of Health-Vital Statistics
Capitol Complex
505 East King Street, #102
Carson City, NV 89710
775-687-4480
Marriage: Contact county
Birth and death: 1911

New Hampshire
Bureau of Vital Records
Health and Human Services Building
6 Hazen Drive
Concord, NH 03301
603-271-4654
Marriage, birth, and death: 1640–

New Jersey
State Department of Health
Bureau of Vital Statistics
P. O. Box 370
Trenton, NJ 08625
609-292-4087
Marriage, birth and death: 1878–

For earlier dates, contact:
Ney Jersey Department of
State Division of Archives
and Records Management
P. O. Box 307
Trenton, NJ 08625-0307

New Mexico
Vital Statistics
Health Services Division
P. O. Box 26110
Santa Fe, NM 87502
505-827-2338
Marriage: Contact county
Birth and death: 1880–

New York

Vital Records Section
P. O. Box 2602
Albany, NY 12220
518-474-3075
Marriage, birth, and death: 1880–

For records before this date, contact the Registrar of Vital Statistics in each city and for records pertaining to New York City, contact:
Office of Vital Records
Department of Health
125 Worth Street, Box 4
New York, NY 10013
212-788-4520
http://www.ci.nyc.ny.us/health

North Carolina

Vital Records Section
P. O. Box 29537
Raleigh, NC 27626
919-733-3526
Marriage: 1962–
Birth: 1913–
Death: 1946–

Death records from 1913–1945 are at:
North Carolina State Archives

109 East Jones Street
Raleigh, NC 27601
919-733-3526
http://schs.state.nc.us/SCHS

North Dakota

Division of Vital Records
State Capitol
600 East Boulevard Avenue
Bismarck, ND 58505
701-328-2360
Marriage: 1925–
Birth and death: 1893–

Ohio

Vital Statistics
Department of Health
P. O. Box 15098
Columbus, OH 43215
614-466-2531
Marriage: 1849–
Birth: 1908–
Death: 1936

Earlier records are at:
Ohio Historical Society
Archives Library
1985 Velma Avenue
Columbus, OH 43211

Oklahoma

Vital Records Section
State Department of Health
1000 Northeast 10th Street
P. O. Box 53551
Oklahoma City, OK 73152
405-271-4040
Marriage: at county
Birth and death: 1908–

Oregon

Oregon Health Division
Vital Statistics Section
P. O. Box 14050
Portland, OR 97293
503-731-4095
http://www.ohd.hr.state.or.us
Marriage: 1906–
Birth and death: 1903–

Pennsylvania

Division of Vital Records
State Department of Health
Central Building
101 South Mercer Street
P. O. Box 1528
New Castle, PA 16103
724-656-3100
Marriage: 1941–
Birth and death: 1906–

Rhode Island

Division of Vital Records
Department of Health
Cannon Building, #101
3 Capital Hill
Providence, RI 02908
401-277-2811
Marriage, birth, and death: 1853–

For records 100 years or less,
write above; for earlier ones
contact:
State Archives
337 Westminister Street
Providence, RI 02903

South Carolina

Office of Vital Records
Department of Health and
Environmental Control
2600 Bull Street
Columbia, SC 29201
803-734-4830
Marriage: 1950–
Birth and death: 1915–

South Dakota
Department of Health
Vital Records
523 East Capitol
Pierre, SC 57501
605-733-3355
http://www.state.sd.us/doh/
vitalrec/vital.htm
Marriage, birth, and death: 1905–

Tennessee
Vital Records
Department of Health and
Environment
421 5th Avenue, North
Nashville, TN 37247
615-741-1763
http://www.state.tn.us/health/vr/
index.html
Marriage: Last 50 years
Birth and death: 1914-

For earlier records, contact:
Tennessee Library
Archives Division
Nashville, TN 37243

Texas
Bureau of Vital Statistics
Department of Health
P. O. Box 12040
Austin, TX 78711
512-458-7111

http://www.tdh.state.tx.us/bvs
Marriage: 1966–
Birth and death: 1903–

Utah
Bureau of Vital Records
Utah Department of Health
288 North 1460 West
P. O. Box 141012
Salt Lake City, UT 84114
801-538-6105
hlunix.ex.state.ut.us/bvr/home.html
Marriage: 1978–
Birth and death: 1905–

Vermont
Department of Health
Vital Records Section
P. O. Box 70
Burlington, VT 05402
802-863-7275
Keeps only last 10 years of records

For earlier records:
Division of Public Records
US Route 2-Middlesex
Drawer 33
Montpelier, VT 05633
Marriage: 1857–
Birth and death: 1760–

Virginia
Division of Vital Records
State Health Department
P. O. Box 1000
Richmond, VA 23218
804-225-5000
Marriage, birth, and death: 1853

Washington
Vital Records
1112 South Quince
P. O. Box 9709
Olympia, WA 98507
360-236-4300
http://www.doh.wa.gov/Topics/
chs-cert. html

Marriage: 1968–
Birth and death: 1907–

West Virginia
Vital Registration Office
Division of Health
State Capital Complex
Building 3
Charleston, WV 25305
304-558-2931
Marriage: 1921
Birth and death: 1917

Wisconsin
Vital Records
1 West Wilson Street
P. O. Box 309
Madison, WI 53701
608-266-1371
http://www.dhfs.state.wi.us/
vitalrecords/index.htm
Marriage: Many dating to 1836,
complete starting 1907–
Birth and death: Many dating to
1856, complete starting 1907–

Wyoming
Vital Records Services
Hathaway Building
Cheyenne, WY 82002
307-777-7591
Marriage: 1941–
Birth and death: 1909–

CANADA

Alberta
Alberta Health
Vital Statistics
P. O. Box 2023
Edmonton, Alberta, T5J 4W7
403-427-2683
Marriage, birth, and death: 1898–
Some birth records date back to 1853
Some death records date back to 1893

British Columbia
Division of Vital Statistics
Ministry of Health
P. O. Box 9657
Stn. Provincial Government
Victoria, B. C., V8W9P3
250-952-2681
Records from 1872–
Some baptismal that date back to
1849

Manitoba
Vital Statistics
Consumer and Corporate
Affairs
254 Portage Avenue
Winnipeg, Manitoba
R3C0B6
Marriage, birth, and death: 1882–

New Brunswick
The Registrar General
Vital Statistics Division
P. O. Box 6000
Fredericton, N.B., E3B 5H1
506-453-2385
Marriage, birth, and death: 1920–

For selected earlier New
Brunswick county records,
contact:
The Provincial Archives
P. O. Box 6000
Fredericton, N.B. E3B 5H1
506-453-2122

Newfoundland
Registrar General
Vital Statistics Division
Dpt. of Government
Services
Confederation Building
5 Mews Place
P. O. Box 8700
St. John's, Newfoundland,
A1B 4J6
709-729-3065
Birth, marriage, death: 1892–

For earlier church records,
contact:
Provincial Archives of
Newfoundland and Labrador
Colonial Building
Military Road
St. John's, Newfoundland,
A1C 2C9

Northwest Territories
Registrar General
Vital Statistics
Department of Health Services
P. O. Box 1320
Yellowknife, N.W.T., X1A 2L9
867-873-7404
Birth, marriage, death: 1925–

Nova Scotia
Deputy Registrar General
P. O. Box 157
Halifax, Nova Scotia, B3J 2M9
902-424-4380
Birth and death: 1908–
Marriage: 1907–

For earlier birth and death
records, and marriage records
from the late 1700s to 1907,
contact:
Public Archives of Nova Scotia
6016 University Avenue
Halifax, N. S. B3H 1W4

Ontario
Registrar General
189 Red River Road
P. O. Box 4600
Thunder Bay, Ontario, P7B 6Lb
416-325-8305
Birth: 1896–
Marriage: 1911–
Death: 1921–

For earlier records, contact:
Archives of Ontario
77 Grenville Street
Toronto, Ontario M7A 2R9

Prince Edward Island
Director of Vital Statistics
Department of Health and
Social Sciences
P. O. Box 2000
Charlottetwon, P.E.I, C1A 7N8
902-368-4420
Birth, marriage, death: 1906–

For earlier records, contact:
Public Archives and Records
P. O. Box 1000
Charlottetwon, P.E.I. Ci1A 7M4
902-368-4290

Quebec

Directeur de l'Etat Civil
Direction generale de
l'enregistrement
Ministere de la Justice
205 Montmagny St.
Quebec, GIN 4T2
418-643-3900
Birth, marriage, death: 1900–

For records dating from the
early 1600s, contact:
Archives National du Quebec
Pavillon Louis-Jacques Casault
Cite universitaire
1210, aveneu de Seminaire
Sainte-Foye, Quebec
GiV4M1

Saskatchewan

Vital Statistics Branch
1942 Hamilton
Regina, Saskatchewa S4P 3V7
800-548-1179
Birth, marriage, death: 1920–
(Some earlier records)

Yukon Territory

Vital Statistics
Government of the Yukon
Territory
P. O. Box 2703
Whitehorse, Yukon Y1A 2C6
403-667-5207
Birth, marriage, death: 1924–
Birth record index: 1900–1924

Genealogical Magazines, E-Zines, and Web Sites

Magazines

Ancestry
Ancestry, Inc.
P. O. Box 990
Orem, UT 84059-0990
http://www.ancestry.com

A bi-monthly, *Ancestry* has timely feature stories and columns on ethnic sources, beginner's advice, research fundamentals, library sources, and technology. *Ancestry* also prints book reviews and case studies where readers reveal their "brick walls" and solutions.

Everton's Genealogical Helper
P. O. Box 368
Logan, UT 84321
http://www.everton.com/

This magazine manages to interest both the novice and the expert with its coverage of classic and emerging genealogical topics. It also lists the newest field publications with a short content description. Nicely indexed, *Everton's* is filled with surnames that are being worked on. Get a free magazine copy by e-mailing *Everton's* at its web site and take a look at its databases! A genealogical classic.

HeritageQuest
P. O. Box 329
Bountiful, UT 84011

Another all-around magazine, *HeritageQuest* typically has twenty articles in each issue to satisfy all levels of genealogical expertise. You can also subscribe to the GenealogyBulletin, a weekly e-zine. Ask for a free sample of each when contacting *HeritageQuest*.

National Genealogical Society Quarterly
101 Newbury Street
Boston, MA 02116

The grandaddy of genealogical publications, the *National Genealogical Society Quarterly* has been publishing U.S. genealogical, methodology updates, book reviews, and source materials since 1912. The journal strives to keep a balance between scholarship and practical "how-to" and promises to "prove that the best-done begats are never boring." Members of the Society get this publication free.

The Genealogical Journal
P. O. Box 1144
Salt Lake City, UT 84110

If you are looking for a "how to" magazine, this is the one! Mostly written by professional genealogists, *The Genealogical Journal* covers both U.S. and international genealogical topics.

E-ZINES

Don't forget free electronic magazines, commonly known as e-zines. Most are weekly. Subscribe by e-mail, and if you don't like the magazine, "unsubscribe." It's that easy! Here are a few:

- Ancestor News (http://www.ancestornews.com/)
- Eastman's Online Genealogy ((http://www.ancestry.com/columns/eastman/index.htm)
- English and Welsh Roots (http://globalgenealogy.com/gaz36.htm)

- Family Tree Finders (send e-mail to: join-family-tree-finders@gt.sodamail.com
- Irish Origins (http://globalgenealogy.com/gaz37.htm)

WEB SITES

http://www.RootsWeb.com

At present, RootsWeb hosts more than 2,700 websites and 3,600 mailing lists. It also sponsors volunteer genealogy programs, such as USGenWeb and WorldGenWeb, that enable users to access information from more than 2,000 web sites made by field experts. WorldGenWeb even has one devoted to genealogy in Antarctica! Besides being able to search e-mail archives, you can conduct research by using the Social Security Death Index and Roots' databases for surname or specific place.

For instance, the state of Kansas section enables you to search for Kansas surnames, people in Kansas currently being researched, or books in the Library of Congress with the subject of Kansas and genealogy. You can also view listings of historical societies, courthouses, city and county histories, Kansas census information, Kansas military listings, family history centers, and on-line library catalogs. There are even articles on the earthquake history of Kansas or the history of brewing in Kansas!

http://www.ancestry.com

The collection of online articles alone makes this site worth the look. Several genealogical columnists are featured, including the well-known Myra Vanderpool Gormley. Ancestry.com doesn't list just a few articles—its offering goes back for years! Recent articles by Gormley, for instance, include, "Books on CD: Genealogy Materials at Bargain Prices," "Canada Opens

Pier 21—Its Ellis Island," and "Finding 19th-Century British Ancestors."

Ancestry.Com offers unlimited access to its millions of records with more being added daily. It has the following databases exclusive to the site:

- Census indexes
- The Periodical Source Index, the largest index of genealogical and historical articles in the world
- Marriage records for 25 states
- The American Genealogical-Biographical Index that has records for persons whose names have appeared in printed genealogical records and family histories
- UMI Obituaries (full text obituaries reported in 85 newspapers since 1990)

http://www.cyndislist.com

A clearinghouse of genealogical web sites, Cyndi's is a one-stop genealogical searching trip! With more than 100 categories, Cyndi's can take you to where you want to go. Her categories, updated regularly, include specific countries, special challenges, books, research services, schools, specific religions, family home pages, dictionaries, on-line starting points, and many, many more. There's even one for myths, hoaxes, and scams.

Of special help is her section on databases, search sites, and surname lists. These are sorted by commercial, general, locality specific, military, people and families, records, and societies and groups. The databases on localities concentrate on the British Isles and are mostly surname listing from specific places, such as Bedfordshire (England) or Carmarthenshire (Wales). The records section varies from actual records to merely guidelines. This section grows daily.

GENEALOGICAL PUBLISHERS

Boyd Publishing Company
P. O. Box 367
Milledgeville, GA 31061
http://www.home.net/~gac/index.html

Genealogical Publishing Company
1001 N. Calvert Street
Baltimore, MD 21202
800-296-6687
http://www.genealogybookshop.com/genealogybookshop/
index.html

Genealogy Unlimited
P. O. Box 537
Orem, UT 84059
800-666-4363
http://lusers.ifsnet.com/~genum

Heritage Book News
1540-E Pointer Ridge Place
Bowie, Maryland 20716
800-398-7709
http://www.heritagebooks.com

BIBLIOGRAPHY

Bentley, Elizabeth. (1998) *The Genealogist's Address Book*. *Baltimore: Genealogical Publishing*.

Carmack, Sharon. (1998). *A Genealogist's Guide to Discovering Your Female Ancestors*. Whitehall, VA: Betterway.

Colletta, John. (1998). *They Came in Ships: A Guide to Finding Your Immigrant Ancestors's Ship*. Orem, UT: Ancestry.

Daus, Carol. (1998). *Past Imperfect: How Tracing Your Family Medical History Can Save Your Life*. Santa Monica, CA: Santa Monica Press.

Dollarhide, William. (1999). *The Census Book*. Bountiful, UT: Heritage Quest.

Hatcher, Patricia. (1997). *Producing a Quality Family History*. Orem, UT: Ancestry.

Hone, E. Wade. (1998). *Land and Property Research in the United States*. Orem, UT: Ancestry.

Howells, C. (1999). *Cyndi's List: A Comprehensive List of 40,000 Genealogy Sites on the Internet*. Baltimore: Genealogical Publishing.

Lackey, Richard. (1986). *City Your Sources: Manual for Documenting Family Histories and Genealogical Records*. Jackson, MS: University Press of Mississippi, 1986.

Luebking, Sandra (ed). (1997). *The Source: A Guidebook of American Genealogy*. Orem, UT: Ancestry.

Mills, Elizabeth. (1997). *Evidence! Citation and Analysis for the Family Historian*. Genealogical Publishing.

Westin, Jeane. (1999). *Finding Your Roots: How to Trace Your Ancestor's Here and Abroad*. J.P. Tarcher.

Woodtar, Dee. (1999). *Finding a Place Called Home: A Guide to African American Genealogy and Historical Identity*. New York: Random House.

The HandyBook for Genealogists. (1999). Logan, UT: Everton Publishers.

Order Form
1-800-784-9553

	Quantity	Amount
THE BOOK OF GOOD HABITS ($9.95)		
COLLECTING SINS (A NOVEL) ($13)		
HEALTH CARE HANDBOOK ($12.95)		
HELPFUL HOUSEHOLD HINTS ($12.95)		
HOW TO FIND YOUR FAMILY ROOTS AND WRITE YOUR FAMILY HISTORY ($14.95)		
HOW TO WIN LOTTERIES, SWEEPSTAKES . . . ($14.95)		
LETTER WRITING MADE EASY! ($12.95)		
LETTER WRITING MADE EASY! VOLUME 2 ($12.95)		
NANCY SHAVICK'S TAROT UNIVERSE ($15.95)		
OFFBEAT FOOD ($19.95)		
OFFBEAT GOLF ($17.95)		
OFFBEAT MARIJUANA ($19.95)		
OFFBEAT MUSEUMS ($19.95)		
PAST IMPERFECT: HOW TRACING YOUR FAMILY MEDICAL HISTORY CAN SAVE YOUR LIFE ($12.95)		
SILENT ECHOES: DISCOVERING EARLY HOLLYWOOD THROUGH THE FILMS OF BUSTER KEATON ($24.95)		
WHAT'S BUGGIN' YOU? ($12.95)		

> **Shipping & Handling:**
> 1 book $3.00
> Each additional
> book is $ .50

Subtotal	
Shipping and Handling (see left)	
CA residents add 8.25% sales tax	
TOTAL	

Name _____

Address _____

City_____ State _____ Zip _____

❏ Visa   ❏ MasterCard   Card Number _____

Signature _____

❏ Enclosed is my check or money order payable to:

Santa Monica Press LLC
P.O. Box 1076
Santa Monica, CA 90406
www.santamonicapress.com
smpress@pacificnet.net

1-800-784-9553

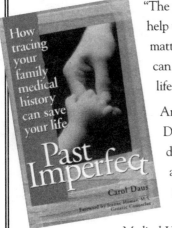